1 MONTH OF
FREE
READING

at

www.ForgottenBooks.com

By purchasing this book you are eligible for one month membership to ForgottenBooks.com, giving you unlimited access to our entire collection of over 1,000,000 titles via our web site and mobile apps.

To claim your free month visit:
www.forgottenbooks.com/free768043

ISBN 978-0-484-33162-3
PIBN 10768043

Abraham Lincoln'
Contemporaries

Rutherford B. Hayes

xcerpts from newspapers and oth
sources

An Index and List of the

Pamphlets and Periodicals

Collected by
RUTHERFORD BIRCHARD HAYES

An Index and List
of the
PAMPHLETS
AND
PERIODICALS

Collected by

Rutherford Birchard Hayes

Nineteenth President of the United States

THE HAYES MEMORIAL LIBRARY
SPIEGEL GROVE STATE PARK
FREMONT, OHIO

Published by

The Ohio State Archaeological and Historical Society

Columbus, Ohio

1935

Printed by
HAIGH & HAIGH, INC., TOLEDO
1935

INTRODUCTION

The Hayes Memorial Library at Fremont, Ohio, is the property of the State of Ohio by deed of gift to the State from Colonel Webb C. Hayes, son of President Rutherford B. Hayes. It is controlled and managed for the State by the Ohio State Archaeological and Historical Society which has its headquarters in Columbus, Ohio.

The Rutherford B. Hayes and Lucy Webb Hayes Foundation is an independent, privately endowed Association formed to perpetuate the name and fame of Rutherford B. Hayes and his wife, Lucy Webb Hayes. The Foundation is, in part, furthering the purposes for which it was formed by assisting the Hayes Memorial Library to place its material and facilities at the service of competent historical scholars and research workers. It plans to aid in the development and enlargement of the original and secondary source material in the Hayes Memorial Library, particularly with respect to the Reconstruction Period in American history, and hopes that ultimately the Memorial Library will become one of the important centers of source material covering that period.

The Life of Rutherford Birchard Hayes, by Charles Richard Williams, was published in two volumes by Houghton Mifflin Company in 1914. This edition was followed by a new edition published by the Ohio State Archaeological and Historical Society. *The Diary and Letters of Rutherford Birchard Hayes,* edited by Charles Richard Williams, was published in five volumes by the Ohio State Archaeological and Historical Society between 1922 and 1926. That Society also published an *Illustrated Catalogue of Spiegel Grove State Park, The Hayes Memorial Library and Museum, and the Hayes Homestead* in 1926. At the time these volumes were published the huge mass of Hayes manuscripts was totally unorganized. It was not only unindexed but was in greater part unfiled and unassembled. Williams spent untold hours of the most painstaking labor in finding and assembling the material from which his works above mentioned were prepared and edited.

The Board of Trustees of the Hayes Foundation secured the services of Miss Ruth M. Boring of the Remington Rand, Inc., to arrange, file, and index the mass of Hayes papers, pamphlets and periodicals in the Hayes Memorial Library to make them easily available to research scholars. A portion of the admirable work done by Miss Boring is shown by the accompanying Index and List which gives some idea of the organized material now available for use. The mass of the material is so great that it would take years to prepare a complete calendar of it. The Index simply mentions the most important events, subjects, and personages with which the material deals. Fuller information on any topic or topics including a previous publication *Letters and Papers* may be secured by communicating with the Hayes Memorial Library at Fremont.

INDEX OF THE PAMPHLET FILE OF THE HAYES MEMORIAL LIBRARY, FREMONT, OHIO

ଔ

The General Pamphlet File at the Hayes Memorial Library contains about 17,000 pamphlets.

They cover a wide range of subjects, indicating the scope of Rutherford B. Hayes' interests and activities. They include many pamphlets which are exceedingly rare. Some may even be the only surviving copies.

The indexes do not completely cover either the subjects or the items included in the collection. They are indicative of the contents and scope of the material. They include the following groups:

A. GENERAL SUBJECT LIST

Abolition
Academy of Natural Sciences
Acts and Resolutions of the 43rd Congress 1873-4
Adirondacks
Africa
    Colonization
    Columbian Exposition
    South
African Exploration
African Habits
African Methodist Episcopal Church
African Problem
Agricultural Subjects
    Education
    Experimental Stations
    Fairs
    Machinery
Agriculture.
    American—General
    California
    Canada
    Department—U. S.
    France
    Georgia
    Handbooks
    International
    Irrigation
    Kansas
    Maine
    Ohio
    Products
    Statistics
Alabama, State of
    Auditor's Reports
    Census Statistics—U. S.
    Convict System
    Education
    Elections—1874—1875—1876
    Federal Government Relations
    Legislature
    Senatorship Controversy—1875
    Treasurer's Reports
Alabama Claims
    See also Geneva Awards
Alaska, Territory of
    Central Railway
    Customs District
    Data—Miscellaneous
    Description
    Difficulties at Sitka 1885

    Geographic Influences
    Glaciers
    Government Publications
    Governor's Reports
    Klondyke Country
    Population
    Presbyterian Missions
    Reports—U. S.
    Surface Features
    Valley of Ten Thousand Smokes
    Volcanoes
    Wealth and Resources
Alaskan Civilization
Alaskan Natural History and Ethnology
Albany County (N. Y.)
    Penitentiary Reports
Albany, City of
    History
    Tourist's Guide
Alexandria (Va.), City of
    Address—Mayor
    Finances
    Schools
Allegheny County (Pa.)
    Centennial
    History
    Republican Executive Committee 1876-7
    Workhouse Reports
Almanacs
    Aetna Life
    Amazon Insurance Co.
    Ayer's American
    Baltimore Sun
    Capitol
    Chronicle
    Family Christian
    Family Health
    Hamburger Familien Kalender
    Harrison
    Independent
    Jaynes' Medical
    Johnston's
    Josh Billings
    Nast's Illustrated
    New York Tribune
    Philadelphia Public Ledger
    Poor Richard
    Radway's
    Republic
    Safeguard
    Scovell's Farmers and Mechanics

[8]

World War . .
World's Columbian Exposition—1893
Wright, George Frederick
Wyoming, State and Territory of

Yale College
Yellow Fever Epidemics
Yellowstone Park
Yorktown Centennial

B. PERIODICALS OF THE HAYES PERIOD AND AFTER

American Academy of Political and
Social Science
1890-1893 incomplete but includes Vol.
I, no. 1.
American Ancestry
1888.
American Anthropologist
1892; 1905-1922.
American Antiquarian
1878, Vol. I, no. 1, Cleveland, Ohio.
American Antiquarian and Oriental
Journal
1889; 1891 incomplete.
American Bibliopolist
1873-1874; 1876 incomplete.
American Historical Review
American Journal of Psychology
1887, Vol. I, no. 1.
American Missionary (The)
1881-1891.
American Statistical Review
1879, Vol. I, part 1.
An-Archist
January, 1881.
Appalachia
1881-1920 incomplete.
Archaeologist (The)
1893-1895 complete with Vol. I, no. 1.

Buchanan's Journal of Man
1887-1889 incomplete.

Californian (The)
1880.
Civil Service Record
Collector (The)
1883 incomplete.

Danville, Ky., Quarterly Review
1861-1864, Vols. I-IV complete.
Forum (The)
1886-1892 incomplete.

Illinois State Historical Society Journal
1922.

Indian Notes
1924-1930.
International Review
1877-1881.
International Standard
1883-1888.
Iowa Journal of History and Politics
1903—

Journal of American History
Journal of Prison Discipline and
Philanthropy

Magazine of American History
1877-1893.
Magazine of Western History
1886-1887 incomplete.
Michigan History Magazine
1917.
Minnesota History Bulletin
1915-1923 incomplete.
Minnesota History Quarterly
Magazine
1927—
Mississippi Valley Historical Review
1914—

Ohio Archaeological and Historical
Quarterly
Ohio Journal of Science
1915-1921.
Ohio Naturalist
1903-1915 incomplete.

Palimpsest (The)
1929—
Penn Monthly
Potter's American Monthly
1875-1880.

Republic (The)
1876-1877.

United Service (The)
1889-1902.

C. OHIO IMPRINTS

Allen, William
  Inaugural address, 1874.
  Columbus—State Printer.
Andrews, E. B.
  A funeral discourse on the occasion of
    the death of Hon. Ephraim Cutter.
  Marietta—Intelligencer, 1854.

Black, James B.
  Cedar Creek; a poem.
  Cincinnati, 1866.
Blind, Education of
  Annual report of Ohio Institution.
  Columbus—Chas. Scott, 1851.
Briggs, Robert M.
  Resolutions and addresses relative to the
    death of—
  Cincinnati—Robert Clarke & Co., 1869.
Brough, John
  Inaugural address—Governor of Ohio—
    1864.
  Columbus—State Printer.
Brush, S.
  Farewell address—Late President of the
    Franklin County Agricultural Society.
  Columbus—Ohio State Journal, 1854.

Cincinnati and the Miami Country
  Celebration of the 45th anniversary of
    the first settlement.
  Cincinnati—Shreve & Gallagher, 1834.
Coggeshall, William T.
  A discourse on the sound and moral
    advantages of the cultivation of local
    literature.
  Beta Theta Pi Society of Ohio Uni-
    versity.
  Columbus—Follett Foster & Co., 1859.
Comegys, C. G.
  Reminiscenses of the life and public
    services of Edward Tiffin.
  Chillicothe, 1869.
Crabb, W. Darwin
  Biographical sketches of the state offi-
    cers and members of the 60th general
    assembly of the State of Ohio.
  Columbus, 1872.

Deshler, John G.
  A financial system for the "Granger"
    with the argument.
  Columbus—Ohio State Journal Book and
    Job Rooms, 1874.

Doddridge, Joseph
  Logan . . . Chief of the Cayuga nation. . .
    to which is added the dialogue of the
    backwoodsman and the dandy.
  Reprinted from the Virginia Edition of
    1823.
  Cincinnati—Robert Clarke & Co., 1868.

Ewing, Thomas
  England: her present condition and fu-
    ture prospects as one of the powers of
    the earth.
  Cincinnati—R. W. Carroll & Co., 1866.

Fairchild, James H.
  Oberlin: Its origin, progress and results.
    An address prepared for the Alumni
    of Oberlin College.
  Oberlin—R. Butler, 1871.
Friends—Yearly Meeting—Indiana
  Address to the people of the United
    States and to the members of Congress
    in particular in the civilization and
    Christian instruction of the aborigines
    of our country.
  Cincinnati—A. Pugh, 1838.

Giles, John
  Memoirs of odd adventures, strange de-
    liverances, etc., in the capitivity of
    John Giles, Esq.
  Written by himself—1736.
  Reprinted for William Dodge.
  Cincinnati—Spiller and Gates, 1869.
Gnadenhuetten Indian Massacre
  A true history of the massacre of ninety-
    six Christian Indians at Gnadenhuet-
    ten, March 8, 1782.
  New Philadelphia—Ohio Democrat Of-
    fice, 1870.
Grimke, Thomas Smith
  Oration delivered at the ninth anniver-
    sary celebration of the Erodelphian
    Society of Miami University.
  Cincinnati—Truman and Smith, 1834.
Gustin, M. E.
  Exposé—Experience and confession of a
    Granger.
  Dayton—Christian Publishing Co., 1875.

Hall, James
  The West: Its soil, surface and produc-
    tions.
  Cincinnati—Robinson and Jones, 1848.

Hall, William
  The Abomination of Mormonism exposed.
  Cincinnati—I. Hart & Co., 1852.
Halstead, Murat
  The war claims of the South. . . . The candidacy of Hayes . . . and letters addressed to the editor of the New York *World* replying to Governor Tilden.
  Cincinnati—R. Clarke, 1876.
Hazen, W. B.
  Our barren lands. The interior of the United States west of the one-hundredth meridian and east of the Sierra Nevadas.
  Cincinnati—R. Clarke & Co., 1875.

Johnston, William
  Speech of Judge Johnston at Delaware, Ohio, being a brief review of the claims of S. J. Tilden as set forth in the Cincinnati Enquirer before his nomination.
  Cincinnati—R. Clarke & Co., 1876.
Johnston, William
  Speech on Rutherford B. Hayes at Avondale, Ohio, July 21, 1876.
  Cincinnati—R. Clarke & Co., 1876.

King, John B.
  Address to the people of the United States in behalf of the preservation of the American Union.
  Irontown—Journal Job Office, 1869.
King, John W.
  Federalism: or the question of exclusive power, the true issue in the present monetary and political discussion in the United States—2nd edition.
  Cincinnati—U. P. James, 1841.

Lake Erie, Battle of
  An account of the organization and proceedings of the Monument Association . . . and celebration of the 45th anniversary.
  Sandusky—H. D. Cooke, 1858.
Laws of Ohio
  Relative to the town of Rossville, and ordinances passed by the mayor and council of Rossville. . . .
  Rossville—J. M. Christy, 1842.

Methodist Episcopacy
  A tract, containing authentic documents from the writings of the Rev. Messrs.

John and Charles Wesley, Rev. Dr. Coke, Bishop White, and others, submitted to the candid consideration of the reader by a churchman.
  Delaware—Ezra Griswold, 1823.
Miami University
  Baccalaureate addresses.
  George Junkin, 1842, 1843, 1844.
  Rossville—J. M. Christy.
Miami University
  Catalogs, 1842, 1843, 1853, 1868, 1870, 1871, 1872—Annual.
  Catalogs, 1840—3rd Triennial.
Miami University
  Erodelphian Society.
  Addresses, 1834, 1837, 1838, 1839, 1840, 1843.
Miami University
  Inauguration addresses of R. L. Stanton . as president.
  Oxford—Richard Butler, 1867.
Miami University
  Miscellaneous addresses. .
  (1) R. H. Bishop.
    Hamilton—Joseph C. Monfort, 1835.
  (2) James H. Bacon.
    Cincinnati—William L. Mendenhall, 1843.
Miami University
  Society of Inquiry on Missions.
  (1) Address on the nature and cultivation of the missionary spirit, by Chauncey N. Olds.
    Oxford—R. H. Bishop, 1837.
  (2) Address by J. Claybough.
    Rossville—J. M. Christy, 1842.
Moulton, G. W.
  The review of General Sherman's memoirs examined chiefly in the light of its own evidence.
  Cincinnati—Robert Clarke & Co., 1875.

Neff Petroleum Company
  Prospectus; with geological reports.
  Gambier—Western Episcopalian, 1866.
New Jerusalem—Doctrines of
  Circular to the individual receivers of the doctrines of New Jerusalem westward of the Allegheny Mountains.
  Cover and title page missing but circular is dated at Cincinnati, November 26, 1833.

Oberlin College
  Coeducation of the sexes as pursued in

Oberlin College.
Address by J. H. Fairchild, 1867.

Oberlin College
Oberlin: Its origin, progress and results. An address prepared for the alumni of Oberlin College by President Fairchild.
Oberlin—R. Butler, 1871.

Ohio Biography
The Firelands Pioneer. New series, Vols. I-III.
Published by the Firelands Historical Society, Norwalk.

Ohio Postoffices
In alphabetical order by counties . . . and an alphabetical list of towns.
Columbus—Richard Nevins, 1861.

Ohio State Board of Agriculture
Tenth annual report, 1835.
Chillicothe—Baker & Miller, 1856.

Ohio State Library
Catalog, December, 1837.
Zachariah Mills, Librarian.
Columbus—S. Medary, 1837.
Also December, 1842.

Perry, Aaron F.
Address delivered before the graduating class and pupils of Esther Institute.
Columbus—Greener & Scott, 1857.

Prentice, George Dennison
A memorial address by Henry Watterson.
Cincinnati—R. Clarke & Co., 1870.

Presbyterian Church—Miami, Ohio
Manifesto and declaration of the Free Associate Presbytery of Miami.
Xenia—Curry & McBratney, 1843.

Railroads—Cleveland, Coshocton and Zanesville
Report—1853.

Railroads—Toledo, Norwalk & Cleveland Railroad Company
Exhibit of the condition and prospects.
Cleveland—Sanford and Hayward, 1852.

Reed, Henry
The public debt: what to do with it.
Cincinnati—R. Clarke & Co., 1868.

Religion and the State
A centennial sermon, by Frederick Merrick.
Cincinnati—Hitchcock & Walden, 1875.

Religious Sects—Disciples of Christ

Historical sketches of the Disciple Churches in Licking County, Ohio, by Jacob Winter, Pioneer Paper, no. 53.
Newark—Clark and King, 1869.

Religious Sects—Episcopal
The state and prospects of our Church as indicated by her last general convention, by Dudley A. Tyng.
Cincinnati—C. F. Bradley, 1854.

Religious Sects—Methodist
The bold frontier preacher. A portraiture of Rev. William Cravens, of Virginia.
Cincinnati—Hitchcock & Walden, 1869.

Religious Sects—Universalists
The Universalist preacher and evangelical repository. . . in defense of Universalism. Vol. II, nos. 2 and 3.
Dayton—John Wilson, 1840.

Riverside, Ohio
Laws and ordinances.
Cincinnati—R. Clarke & Co., 1868.

Rossville, Ohio
Laws of Ohio relative to the town of Rossville, and ordinances passed by the mayor and council of Rossville.
Rossville—J. M. Christy, 1842.

Schools and Colleges
Huron Institute, Milan, Ohio.
Catalogue of officers and students, 1848-1849.
Clark Waggoner, job printer, 1849.

Scott, J. W.
A presentation of causes tending to fix the position of the future great city of the world in the central plains of North America.
Toledo, 1868.

Shakers
A brief exposition of the established principles of the United Society of Believers called Shakers.
Watervliet — Richard McNemar and David Spinning, 1832.

Sheldon Family in America
Genealogy.
Henry Olcott Sheldon.
Loudonville, 1855.

Smith, George B.
The Bible: is it a guide to Heaven?
Sandusky, 1854.

Spalding, Rufus
Oration with an account of the celebration of the anniversary of the battle

of Lake Erie and laying the corner-stone of the monument.
Sandusky—H. D. Cooke, 1859.

Texas—Western
The Australia of America; or the place to live, by a six-year resident.
Cincinnati—E. Mendenhall, 1860.

Todd, Charles S. (and Benjamin Drake)
Sketches of the civil and military services of William Henry Harrison.
Cincinnati—U. P. James, 1840.

Toledo, Norwalk & Cleveland Railroad Company
Exhibit of the condition and prospects.
Cleveland—Sanford and Hayward, 1852.

Universalist Preacher and Evangelical Repository

In defense of Universalism. Vol. II, nos. 2 and 3.
Dayton—John Wilson, 1840.

Vananda, C. A.
A discourse; delivered to the Ross County Volunteers on Sunday, April 21, 1861 . . . Chillicothe, Ohio.
Greenfield—Republican Office, 1861.

Wabash and Erie Canal
Speech of W. W. Griffith in the Ohio legislature.
Toledo—Daily Commercial, 1871.

Western Art Union
Transactions 1849 and 1850.
Cincinnati—Daily Times Job Office.

Whittlesey, Charles
Report of explorations in the mineral regions of Minnesota, 1848, 1859, 1864.
Cleveland, 1866.

D. EARLY AND RARE PAMPHLETS

Abingdon, Earl of
Observations on Burke's Letter.
Fourth edition — also includes Second Thoughts or Observations, 1777.
Oxford—W. Jackson, 1777.

Abingdon, Earl of
Thoughts on the letter of Edmund Burke, Esq., to the Sheriffs of Bristol on the affairs of America.
Oxford—W. Jackson, 1777.

Adams, John
History of the dispute with America; from its origin in 1754, written in the year 1774 by John Adams.
London—J. Stockdale, 1784.

Adams, John Quincy
Addresses in the Congress of the United States and the Funeral Solemnities on the death of John Quincy Adams.
Washington—J. & G. S. Gideon, 1848.

Adams, John Quincy
Eulogy by H. M. Brackenridge.
Pittsburgh, 1848.

Adams, John Quincy
The Jubilee of the Constitution.
New York—Samuel Colman, 1839.

Adams, John Quincy
Letters on the Entered Apprentice's Oath.

Boston—Young Men's Anti-Masonic Association, 1833.

Adams, John Quincy
An oration addressed to the citizens of the town of Quincy on the Fourth of July, 1831.
Boston—Richardson, Lord & Holbrook, 1831.

Agricola's Grain Question—An Anachronism (Specie Payments)

Albany Academy
Celebration of the Semi-Centennial Anniversary, June 23, 1863.
Albany—Joel Munsell, 1863.

Albany County (N. Y.) Penitentiary
Rules, regulations and by laws.
Albany—Joel Munsell, 1868.

Alcott, Louisa M.
Proverb Stories.
Boston—Loring, 1868.

Allan, John
Memoir with a Genealogy.
Albany—Joel Munsell, 1867.

Allen, William
Campaign Melodies.
Springfield, Ill., 1876.

Alvord, J. W.
Historical Address . . . at the celebration

of the second centennial anniversary of the first settlement of the town of Stamford.
New York—S. Davenport, 1842.

American Art-Union
Bulletins, 1848, 1849, 1850, 1851.
New York.

American Art-Union
Transactions for the years 1848, 1849.
New York—George F. Nesbit.

American Bankers Association
Proceeding 1876 and 1877.

American Institutions for the Insane
Project of a law to determine the legal relations of the insane, adopted by the Association of Medical Superintendents.
Boston, 1868.

Ammen, Daniel
Six pamphlets dealing with the problem of an Interoceanic Canal, 1878-1889.

Ancient and Honorable Artillery Company
Boston, Massachusetts, 231st Anniversary, 1869.
Boston—Rockwell & Churchill, 1870.

Anderson, Ephraim F.
Memorial Address — Antietam National Cemetery, May 30, 1870.
Baltimore, Md.—John Cox.

Apache Indian Outrages
Memorial and Affidavits showing outrages perpetrated in the territory of Arizona during the years 1869 and 1870.
San Francisco, Calif.—Frances and Valentine, 1871.

Arizona Territory
Information to promote Immigration.
San Francisco, Calif.—Frances and Valentine, 1871.

Armstrong, Edward
Address before the Historical Society of Pennsylvania in celebration of the 169th anniversary of the landing of William Penn.
Philadelphia—J. Pennington, 1852.

Arnold, L. M.
The History of the Origin of all Things.
The History of the Word, 1852.

Auxiliary Colonization Society of Lexington and Fayette Counties
Second Annual Report of the Managers of the Lexington and Fayette County Auxiliary Colonization Society, made at the annual meeting, July 8, 1828.
Presented to H. Clay by W. O. Leary.
Lexington, Ky. — Smith and Palmer, 1828.

Ayer's American Almanac
For the use of Farmers, Planters, Mechanics, Mariners and all Families, 1862 and 1870.
Lowell, Massachusetts.

Bacon, Leonard
Sketch of the life and public service of Hon. James Hillhouse of New Haven.
New Haven, 1860.

Baldwin, Samuel M. and Worley, F. W.
Three Thousand Dollars a Year.
Moving Forward, or How We Got There.
The Complete Liberation of all the People.
Abridged from the advance Sheets of a History of Industrial and Governmental Reforms in the United States to be published in the year 2001 by Benefice.
1890.

Banking Systems—Massachusetts
Bank Bills or Paper Currency, and the banking system of Massachusetts by a Conservative.
Boston—Little, Brown & Co., 1856.

Banks—National
Proceedings of the Convention of National Banks, and remarks of Hon. Thomas Coleman.
Syracuse, N. Y.—Journal Book and Job Office, 1865.

Banneker, Benjamin
A sketch of the life of—from notes taken in 1836.
Maryland Historical Society, 1854.

Banvard, John
Description of Banvard's panorama of the Mississippi River, painted on three miles of canvas exhibiting a view of country 1200 miles in length, extending from the mouth of the Missouri River to the City of New Orleans; being by far the largest picture ever executed by man.
Boston—J. Putnam, 1847.

Baptists
The Annual Register of the Baptist Denomination in North America to the first of November, 1790. Containing

an account of the Churches and their Constitutions, Ministers, Members, Associations, their Plan and Sentiments, Rule and Order, Proceedings and Correspondence. Also Remarks upon Protestant Religion humbly offered to the Public by John Asplund, 1791.

Barnes, Albert
Life at Three-Score. 6th edition.
Philadelphia — Presbyterian Publishing Company, 1859.

Barron, John
Facts relating to North-Eastern Texas. Condensed from notes made during a tour through that portion of the United States for the purpose of examining the country as a field for emigration.
London—Simpkin, Marshall & Co., 1849.

Bascom, Henry B.
Report of the Committee on Organization . . . of the Methodist Episcopal Church in the Southern and Southwestern States.
Louisville, Ky.—Prentice and Wissinger, 1845.

Beigel, Herman
The examination and confession of certain witches at Chelmsford in the County of Essex. Communicated and prefaced by Herman Beigel.
Original pamphlet, 1556.
Published by Dr. Beigel, 1864.

Bemis, George
American. Neutrality.
Boston—Little, Brown and Co., 1866.

Benham, Martin
The German Astronomer and Cosmographer of the times of Columbus, by John G. Norris.
Baltimore—Maryland Historical Society, 1855.

Benson, Egbert
Vindication of the Captors of Major Andre, New York, 1817.
Sabin reprint no. 3, 1865.

Berea College
How to start a college; or where can collegiate investments be made which shall be permanent, safe and profitable?
1872.

Bible—Publication and Distribution
Address of the Managers of the Bible Society of Virginia to the Public.
Richmond—Samuel Pleasants, 1814.

Bigelow, Timothy
Dedication of a Monument in his honor at Worcester, Massachusetts, April 19, 1861.
Boston—John Wilson & Son, 1861.

Billings, Josh
Josh Billing's Farmer's Allminax for 1873
New York—G. W. Carleton, 1873

Bingham, John A.
Argument—Trial of the Conspirators for the Assassination of President Lincoln.
1865, autographed.

Binney, William
Proceedings of the city council of Providence on the death of Abraham Lincoln.
Providence, R. I.—Knowles, Anthony & Co., 1865.

Bishop, J. P.
(1) The Southern Question. A view of the policy and constitutional powers of the President as to the Southern States.
(2) Legal View of the Presidential Conflict of 1876.
(3) Supplement to (2).
Cleveland, Ohio—Fairbanks & Co., 1877.

Blair, Frank P.
The destiny of the races of this continent. An address before the Mercantile Library Association of Boston.
Washington—Buell & Blanchard, 1859.

Blasphemy
Report of the Attorney of the Commonwealth at the trial of Abner Kneeland for Blasphemy in the Municipal and Supreme Courts in Boston.
January and May, 1834.
Boston—Beals, Homer & Co.

Bleeker, Leonard (Capt.)
The order book of Capt. Leonard Bleeker, Major of the Brigade, in the early part of the expedition under General James Clinton against the Indian settlements of Western New York in the campaign of 1779.
New York—Joseph Sabin, 1865.

Bliss, Edward
A brief history of the new gold regions of Colorado Territory; together with hints and suggestions to intending emigrants.
New York—J. W. Amerman, 1864.

Bristol and agent for the colony of New York, etc., in answer to his printed speech said to have been spoken in the House of Commons on the 22nd of March, 1775, by Josiah Tucker.
Second edition, corrected.
Gloucester—R. Raikes, 1775.

Burke, Edmund
Speech of Edmund Burke, Esq., on American Taxation, April 19, 1774.
The second edition.
London—J. Dodsley, 1775.

Burke, Edmund
Speech of Edmund Burke, Esq., on moving his resolutions for conciliation with the colonie, March 22, 1775.
The second edition.
London—J. Dodsley, 1775.

Burns, Robert
Centennial anniversary of the birth of Robert Burns, by the Burns Club of Washington City.
Washington—Joseph Shillington, 1859.

Bush, George
The memorabilia of Swedenborg: or memorable relations of things seen and heard in heaven and hell.
New York—J. Allen, 1846.

Butler, Benjamin F.
The status of the insurgent states, upon the cessation of hostilities. The rights of the disloyal—the duties of the Loyal states.
Speech—Pennsylvania Legislature, 1866.

Butterfield, Carlos
The value of Spanish America to the United States.
The promotion of American Commerce.
How to make the Monroe Doctrine effective.
The extinguishment of the National debt in a few years, etc.
New York—Metropolitan, 1868.

Butterfield, Carlos
His labors in behalf of international prosperity in the American Continent.
By William Henry Shaw.
Washington—J. L. Ginck, 1879.

Byers, S. H. M.
What I saw in Dixie; or sixteen months in rebel prisons.
Dansville—Robbins and Poore, 1868.

Byfield, Nathaniel
An account of the late revolution in New England. . . . Boston, 1869.

New York—Reprinted for Joseph Sabin, 1865.

Cadieux, J. N.
Transition: Prohibition of Alcohol—Socially, Medically, Religiously, and Politically.
Second edition.
Muskegon, Mich., 1880.

Calhoun, John C.
Presenting a condensed history of Political Events from 1811 to 1843.
New York—Harper & Bros., 1843.

California—Los Angeles County
Historical Sketch.
Los Angeles—Louis Lewin & Co., 1876.

California Immigrant Union
Common Sense Applied to the Immigrant Question.
C. T. Hopkins.
San Francisco—Trumbull & Smith, 1869.

California State Agricultural Society
Transactions, 1864-1865.
Sacramento—State Printer, 1866.

Canada—Settlement
Sketches and plans for settling in Upper Canada, a portion of the unemployed labourers of Great Britain and Ireland, by a Settler.
Second edition with additions.
London—J. Harding, 1822.

Canal Projects
James River and Kanawha. Memorial to the delegates of the National Board of Trade.
March, 1870.

Canal Projects
Water communication between the Mississippi and the Lakes.
Memorial to the Congress of the United States in the improvement of the navigation of the Wisconsin and Fox Rivers.
Madison, Wis.—Atwood & Culver, 1870.

Cape Cod
A discourse pronounced at Barnstable on the third of September, 1839, at the celebration of the second centennial anniversary of the settlement of Cape Cod.
Boston—Ferdinand Andrews, 1840.

Cardozo, J. N.
Reminiscenses of Charleston.
Charleston, S. C.—Joseph Walker, 1866.

Carey, Henry C.
Answers to the questions:

What constitutes currency?
What are the causes of unsteadiness in the currency? and What is the Remedy?
Philadelphia—Lea & Blanchard, 1840.

Carey, Henry C.
Financial Crises: Their Causes and Effects.
Philadelphia—H. C. Baird, 1864.

Carey, Henry C.
Money: a lecture delivered before the New York Geographical and Statistical Society.
Philadelphia—H. C. Baird, 1860.

Carpenter, F. D.
. . . A trip to the Yellowstone National Park together with a thrilling account of the capture by the Nez Perces Indians and subsequent escape of the National Park Tourists. . .
Black Earth, Wis.—Burnett & Son, 1878.

Castle, Henry A.
The problem of American distiny—an oration delivered at a celebration of the G. A. R. of Minnesota.
St. Paul, Minn.—Press Printing Company, 1868.

Caton, John Dean
The last of the Illinois and a sketch of the Pottawatomies.
Chicago Historical Society, 1870.

Caves—Knoeppel's Schoharie Cave— New York
New York—W. E. & J. Sibell, 1853.

Centennial Exhibition—Philadelphia, 1876
About fifty pamphlets covering various phases of this first great international exhibition in the United States.

Chicago Union Stock Yards
Jack Wing.
Revised edition, 1866.

Chinese Immigration Question
About fifty pamphlets, some of them probably rare. 1877-1879.

Chinese Repository (The)
Vol. VIII, Dec., 1839, no. 8 pp. 385-440.

Christie's Family Almanac
1853.

Chronicle Almanac, 1868

Cilley, Jonathan
Report of the Committee on the late duel which led to the death of Hon. Jonathan Cilley, 1838.

Civil Service
About 200 pamphlets.
1873-1884.

Civil War
About 500 pamphlets, many of them by eye-witnesses and participants. Some of the local publications are probably rare.

Clark, Hiram C.
An examination and discussion of extraordinary popular delusions concerning the true uses and value of money, collected from many sources.
Jamestown, N. Y.—Journal, 1873.

Clarke, Lewis and Milton
Narratives of the sufferings of Lewis and Milton Clarke, sons of a soldier of the Revolution during a captivity of more than twenty years among the slaveholders of Kentucky, one of the so-called Christian States of North America.
Boston—Bela Marsh, 1854.

Clay, Henry
Report on Public Lands made to Senate, 1832.

Cleveland, Coshocton and Zanesville Railroad Company
Report, 1853.

Coin's Financial School
W. H. Harvey.
Chicago—Coin Publishing Co., 1894.

Coleman, Thomas
Convention of National Banks.
Proceedings and remarks of Mr. Coleman.
Syracuse, N. Y.—Journal Book and Job Office, 1865.

Colonial History
Copies of the two protests against the bill to repeal the American Stamp Act of the last session. With lists of the speakers and voters.
Paris—Chez J. W. Imprimeur, 1766.

Colonial History
Epitaphs from the Old Burying Ground at Dorchester, Massachusetts.
Boston—Highlands, 1869.

Colonial History
A full and impartial account of the Company of the Mississippi. . . projected and settled by M. Law. In French and English.
London—R. Francklin, 1720.

Colonial History
History of the issues of paper money in the American Colonies anterior to the Revolution.
St. Louis, Mo.—Union Print, 1851.

Colonial History
An inquiry, whether the absolute independence of America is not to be preferred to her partial dependence, as most agreeable to the real interest of Great Britain.
Addressed to the people of Great Britain by one of themselves.
London—J. Bew & R. Faulder, 1782.

Colonial History
Justice and policy of the late Act of Parliament for making more effectual provision for the Government of the Province of Quebec, asserted and proved, and the conduct of administration respecting that Province stated and vindicated.
London—J. Wilkie, 1774.

Colonial History
A letter to the Earl of Chatham on the Quebec Bill.
London—T. Cadell, 1774.

Colonial History
A letter to a member of Parliament in the present unhappy dispute between Great Britain and her Colonies. Wherein the supremacy of the former is asserted and proved; and the necessity of compelling the latter to pay due obedience to the sovereign state, is enforced, upon principles of sound policy, reason and justice. . . .
London—J. Walter, 1774.

Colonial History
A letter from a merchant in London to his nephew in North America relative to the present posture of affairs in the Colonies.
London—J. Walter, 1766.

Colonial History
One more letter to the people of England by their old friend.
Policy and peace terms of the French and Indian Wars.
London—Printed for J. Pridden at the Feathers in Fleet Street, 1762.

Colonial History
A prospect of the consequences of the present conduct of Great Britain towards America.
London—J. Almon, 1776.

Colonial History
Speech on the Bill for altering the Charters of the Colony of Massachusetts Bay.
Second edition.
London—T. Cadell, 1774.

Colonial History
A succinct view of the origin of our colonies, with their civil state, founded by Queen Elizabeth, corroborated by succeeding Princes, and confirmed by acts of Parliament; whereby the nature of the Empire established in America, and the error of various hypotheses formed thereupon, may be clearly understood. With observations on the commercial, beneficial, and perpetual union of the colonies with this Kingdom being an extract from an essay lately published, entitled, The Freedom of Speech and Writing, etc.
London, 1766.

Colonial History
Taxation no tyranny; an answer to the resolutions and address of the American Congress.
Third edition.
London—T. Cadell, 1775.

Colonial History
Tyranny unmasked; an answer to a late pamphlet entitled Taxation No Tyranny.
London—Author, 1775.

Colonial History
Voyage of George Clarke, Esq., to America; with introduction and notes by E. B. O'Callaghan.
New York Colonial Tracts, no. II.
Edition—100 copies.

Colorado Board of Immigration
Official information.
Denver, 1872 and 1873.

Columbia, South Carolina
The future manufacturing and commercial centre of the South with some accounts of its foundation, destruction and subsequent rehabilitation and growth, 1871.

Conkling, Roscoe
The statesman, orator, and jurist, and the advocate of freedom, humanity, justice, equal rights.
Washington—National Republican, 1876.

Contested Election—1876
A group of contemporary reports and opinions.

Cooper, Peter
The lives of the presidential candidates, 1876.
New York—American Publishing and Manufacturing Co., 1876.

Copeland, Robert Morris
Essay and plan for the improvement of the city of Boston.
Boston—Lee and Shepard, 1872.

Copley, Josiah
Kansas and the country beyond, on the line of the Union Pacific Railway.
Philadelphia—Lippincott, 1867.

Copper Mines—Connecticut
A history of the copper mines and Newgate Prison at Granby, Connecticut. Also of the captivity of Daniel Hayes, of Granby, by the Indians in 1707.
Hartford, Conn.—Case, Tiffany & Burnham, 1845.

Cowden, John
Commercial freedom for the Mississippi Valley. Report on the gateway to the seas and the reclamation of the lowlands.
Memphis—Tracy & Co., 1876.

Cowden, John
The route to the seaboard. The Mississippi River against transcontinental Railroad.
New Orleans—M. Sagendorph, 1877.

Crane, James M.
The past, the present and the future of the Pacific.
San Francisco—Sterett & Co., 1856.

Creek Indians
The Creek Confederacy and a sketch of the Creek Country.
Georgia Historical Society Collections, Col. III, pt. 1, 1848.

Currency or Money
Its nature and uses, and the effects of the circulation of bank-notes for currency.
By a merchant of Boston.
Boston—Little, Brown & Co., 1855.

Curtis, George T.
Arguments in the Court of Appeals, New York, upon the power of Congress to make United States Treasury Notes a Legal Tender.
New York—Wm. C. Bryant & Co., 1868.

Dahlgren, Madeleine Vinton
Etiquette of Social Life in Washington.
Fourth edition.

Washington—Mohun Brothers, 1876.

Dalrymple, John (Sir)
Three letters from Sir John Dalrymple, Bart . . . to the Right Honourable Lord Viscount Barrington . . . on his Lordship's official conduct.
London—J. P. Coghlan, 1778.

Dalrymple, (J.) and Germaine, (G)
The rights of Great Britain asserted against the claims of America: being an answer to the Declaration of the General Congress.
Third edition with additions.
London—T. Cadell, 1776.

Daviess County—Missouri
Its history, description and resources.
St. Joseph, Mo.—Steam Printing Company, 1875.

Deady, Matthew P.
Roseburg address—touching on history of the Great West.
Portland, Ore.—George S. Heines, 1877.

Dealtry, William
Money, its history, evils and remedy.
Albany, N. Y.—Baker,Taylor, 1858.

De Jarnette, D. C.
Speech on the Monroe Doctrine.
Confederate House of Representatives.
January 30, 1865.

De Kalb, John (Baron)
Memoir of—
Read by J. Spear Smith before Maryland Historical Society, 1858.
Baltimore—J. D. Toy, 1858.

De Peyster, J. Watts
Secession in Switzerland and in the United States compared.
Catskill—Jaesbury, 1864.

Dent, Josiah
Lecture on the Mississippi Valley before the St. Louis Mercantile Library Association.
St. Louis, Mo.—Chambers, Knapp, 1853.

Denver and Rio Grande Railway
First report, 1873.

D'Estaing, Charles Hector (Comte)
The siege of Savannah by the combined American and French forces under command of General Lincoln and Count d'Estaing.
Edition—100 copies, no. 3.
Albany—Joel Munsell, 1866.

Doane, George Washington
Address—The Goodby Heritage of Jerseymen—before New Jersey Historical

Society, 1846.
Second edition, 1848.

Dodge, William Sumner
Oration delivered at Sitka, Alaska.
San Francisco, Cal., 1868.

Donaldson, Thomas
American Colonial History: an address before the Maryland Historical Society.
Baltimore—J. Murphy & Co., 1849.

Dwight, Timothy
A sermon preached at Northampton the 28th of November, 1781: occasioned by the capture of the British army under the command of Lord Cornwallis.
Hartford—Nathaniel Patten.

Eads, James B.
Concession from the Mexican Government to J. B. Eads for the construction of a ship railway across the Isthmus of Tehuantepec.
Washington—National Republican, 1880.

Eads, James B.
Report of General Humphreys, Chief of Engineers (Canal Project) reviewed by James B. Eads.
1874.

Eads, James B.
The Tehuantepec ship-railway. Letter to President Hayes, December 22, 1880.

Eastman, Joseph
Reason or Riot?
An analysis of the principles underlying our system of labor, and the principles involved in determining the value of money.
Chicago, 1878.

Eaton, Dorman B.
Five Pamphlets on Civil Service. 1875-1882.

Election of 1876
A large number of contemporary pamphlets.

Electoral College (The)
By "Jurist."
Washington—McGill & Witherow, 1876.

Eliot, Charles W.
Report on a National University.
1873.

Emancipation
By William E. Channing.
Philadelphia—Eastern Pennsylvania A. S. Society, 1841.

Emerson, Ralph Waldo
Historical discourse on Concord—Sept. 12, 1835.
Reprint.
Boston—W. B. Clarke.

Emma Silver Mining Co.
A statement of facts connected with—
Prepared for the use of the Committee on Foreign Affairs, in the investigation of the connection of Gen. Schenck with said Company.
New York—B. H. Tyrrel, 1876.

Everett, Edward
Eulogy on La Fayette, delivered in Faneuil Hall, at the request of the young men of Boston, September 6, 1834.
Boston — Nathan Hale; and Allen & Ticknor, 1834.

Everett, Edward
An oration delivered at Plymouth, Dec. '22' 1824.
Boston — Cummings, Hilliard & Company, 1825.

Ewart, Charles
Correspondence in reference to the unexpended balance of the Geneva award on the Alabama claims between Charles Ewart and the Hon. William E. Gladstone.
Coatesville, Pa.—R. D. Parkinson, 1877.

Ewing—
An appeal to the people of New Jersey by Ewing.
Camden, N. J.—Hineline & Curtis, 1843.

Fairchild, James H.
Inaugural Address.
Oberlin College—Aug. 22, 1866.
New York—Edward O. Jenkins, 1866.

Fairfax Family
The Fairfaxes in England and America in the 17th and 18th Centuries.
Albany, N. Y.—Joel Munsell, 1868.

Farrell, Ned E.
Colorado, the Rocky Mountain Gem as it is in 1868.
Chicago—Western News Co., 1868.

(Ferguson (Dr.))
Remarks in a pamphlet lately published by Dr. Price, entitled, observations on the nature of Civil Liberty, the principles of Government, and the justice and policy of the war with America.
London—T. Cadell, 1776.

Fisher and Brothers
Farmer's Almanac, 1866.

Fleming, Sandford
Canadian Pacific Railway Reports and Documents in reference to the location of the line and a western terminal harbour.
1878.

Florida—Climate, Soil and Productions
. . . A manual of reliable information concerning the resources of the State and the inducements which it offers to immigrants.
L. F. Dewey & Co., 1868.

Ford's New York and Western Farmer's
Almanac, 1867.

Fort Sumter
The Order of Exercises at the Re-raising of the United States Flag on Fort Sumter, April 14, 1865.

Foster, James S.
Outlines of history of the Territory of Dakota, and emigrant's guide to the free lands of the Northwest.
Yankton—Dakota Territory, 1870.

Franks, David
The New York Directory.
New York—Sheppard & Pollock, 1851.

Freeman, Pliny
Correspondence on National Finance 1862, 1875, 1876.

Friends—Society of
The appeal of the religious society of friends in Pennsylvania, New Jersey, Delaware, etc., in behalf of the colored races.
Philadelphia—Friends Book Store, 1858.

Friendship—Letters of
Letters of gratitude to the Connecticut pleader, the Rev. Joseph Huntington for his letters of friendship to a certain class of gentlemen.
By Impartialis.
Jonathan Edwards' Memo written in title-page.
Hartford—Hudson and Goodwin, 1781.

Gallatin, Albert
Inaugural address on taking the chair as President of the New York Historical Society.
New York—J. P. Wright, 1843.

Gano, John
Biographical Memoirs.
New York—Southwick and Hardcastle, 1806.

Gardner, Daniel
Treatise on the Law of the American Rebellion and our true Policy—Domestic and Foreign.
New York—John W. Amerman, 1862.

Garfield, James A.
Campaign Songs.
New York Republican Central Campaign Club, 1880.

Garfield, James A.—Death
Pamphlets giving speeches, memorial services, etc., 1881.

Garfield and Arthur Song Book
Republican National Committee, 1880.

Garfielde, S.
The Northwest Coast.
A lecture.
Washington—Joseph L. Pearson, 1869.

Garrison, William Lloyd
Letter to colored voters.
September 9, 1876.

Garrison, William Lloyd
Letter to Hon. W. E. Chandler on Southern Policy.
Concord, N. H.—Daily Monitor, Extra, January 21, 1878.

Gayarré, Charles
The financial and political condition of Louisiana.
New Orleans—J. W. Madden, 1874.

Georgia—Civil War
The war history of Company "C", 6th Georgia Regiment.
Wendell D. Croom.
Fort Valley, Georgia, 1879.

Georgia Historical Society Collections
Vol. III, part 1.
Savannah, 1848.

Germans of Oregon
Greetings to President Hayes on his Western Trip. Scrap Book.

Geroon, Paul
Address to the American People compiled from authentical sentences and words of George Washington.
Louisville, Ky., 1875.

Gervinins, G. G.
Introduction to the history of the nineteenth century.
London—H. G. Bohn, 1853.

Gibbons, J. A.
The Kanawha Valley, its resources and developments.
Charleston, W. Va.—Gibbons, Atkinson & Company, 1872.

Gilman, Daniel C.
A historical discourse delivered in Norwich, Connecticut, at the Bicentennial celebration of the settlement of the town.
Second edition.
Boston—Rand & Avery, 1859.

Gilmer, Thomas W.
Letter to a sceptical friend.
Philadelphia, C. 1858.

Girard, Stephen
The will of the late Stephen Girard, Esq. . . . with a short biography of his life.
Philadelphia — Thomas and Robert Desliver, 1832.

Goelet, Francis
Extracts from the journal relating to Boston, Salem, Marblehead, etc., 1746-1750.
Boston—David Clapp & Son, 1870.

Gold Panic—1869
Black Friday, September 24, 1869.
George S. Boutwell.

Gold Regions—Colorado
Denver City and Aurora, the commercial emporium of the Pike's Peak gold regions in 1859.

Goodale, Ebenezer
Record of the proceedings of a general court martial, holden at the courthouse in Salem in the county of Essex, Monday, September 25, 1812, by order of his excellency Caleb Strong, Esq., Governor and Commander in Chief of the militia of the Commonwealth of Massachusetts, in the complaint of Col. Samuel Brimblecom and others against Ebenezer Goodale, Major General. . . .
Title-page torn.
Cambridge—Hilliard and Metcalf, 1812.

Grace, William H.
Grace's Exposure! or unsweetened sugars.
A Compilation and Review of the Great Sugar Frauds on the Government and people.
New York—Randel & Bruno, 1879.

Graham, David
Narrative of the proceedings of the ju-

dicatories of the Reformed Church in North America relative to David Graham.
Pittsburgh—S. Engles & Co., 1811.

Grand Army of the Republic
Several hundred pamphlets relative to the National and State Departments; articles on Civil War battles, campaigns and men by eye witnesses. Much additional material among the books of the library, as well as in the letter file.
1868-1893.

Grant, George W.
Recollections of Ulysses S. Grant.
Philadelphia—Collins, 1885.

Grant, Ulysses S.—Third Term
Address of the Grant Campaign Committee of Louisiana, 1879.
New Orleans—George Ellis and Brother, 1879.

Gray, Francis C.
Prison Discipline in America.
Boston—Freeman & Bolles, 1847.

Gray, W. H.
The moral and religious aspect of the Indian question.
Astoria, Oregon, 1879.

Greeley, Horace
The Greeley Record: showing the opinions and sentiments of Horace Greeley. . . .
Washington Union Republican Executive Committee, 1872.

Green, James W.
The present disturbed condition of the country; its causes and its remedy. The re-establishment of constitutional government—The only mode to avert civil war in the future; a peaceful and permanent solution.
New York—J. J. Little & Co., 1877.

Greene, Nathaniel
Examination of some statements in Bancroft's History of the United States by George Washington Greene.
Boston—Ticknor & Fields, 1866.

Grenville, (G)
The regulations lately made concerning the colonies, and the taxes imposed upon them, considered.
London—J. Wilkie, 1765.

Griffith, James F.
Address from the navigation interest to our national legislators, urging that

Congress preserve the unobstructed navigation of the Mississippi River.
St. Louis—G. Knapp, 1866.

Grover, L. F.
Eligibility of electors of President and Vice-President.
Salem, Oregon—State Printer, 1876.

Hair, R. S.
Actual experiences in southeastern and central Dakota.
Chicago—C. N. Triness, 1885.

Harrison, William Henry
Funeral sermon, delivered in the Presbyterian Church in Washington on the Sabbath after the decease of William Henry Harrison . . . in the presence of President Tyler and members of the cabinet by Rev. Cortlandt Van Rensselaer.
Washington—1841.

Harrison, William Henry
The life of Major - General William Henry Harrison: comprising a brief account of his important civil and military services, and an accurate description of the council at Vincennes with Tecumseh, as well as the victories of Tippecanoe, Fort Meigs and the Thames.
Philadelphia—Grigg & Elliot, 1840.

Harrison Almanac, 1841
New York—J. P. Giffing.

Harrold, John
The capture, imprisonment, escape and rescue of John Harrold. (Southern prison of the Civil War).
Philadelphia — William B. Selheimer, 1870.

Hart, Adolphus M.
History of the discovery of the valley of the Mississippi.
St. Louis, Mo., 1852.

Hart, John
Oration by Governor Parker at the dedication of a monument for John Hart, New Jersey signer of the Declaration of Independence.
Trenton, N. J.—1865.

Harvey, W. H.
See Coin's Financial School.

Haven, Samuel F.
An historical address delivered before the citizens of the town of Dedham . . . being the second centennial anni-versary of the incorporation of the town.
Dedham—H. Mann, 1837.

Hayes, Rutherford B.
About two hundred pamphlets, some about him, some by him.

Haygood, Atticus G.
Speeches and articles on Negro Education, 1883-1888.

Hendricks, Thomas A.
The lives of the presidential candidates, 1876.
New York — American Publishing and Manufacturing Co., 1876·

Henry, James P.
Resources of the State of Arkansas, Etc.
Second edition.
Little Rock—Price and McClure, 1872.

Hillhouse, James
Sketch of the life and public service of—
New Haven, 1860.

Holt, Joseph
Vindication from the foul slanders of traitors . . . acting in the interest of Jefferson Davis.
Second edition, 1866.

Homestead Guide
Describing the great homestead region in Kansas and Nebraska.
Waterville, Kansas—F. G. Adams, 1873.

Hopkins, C. T.
Common sense applied to the immigrant question: showing why the California Immigrant Union was founded and what it expects to do.
San Francisco—Trumbull & Smith, 1869.

Hospital Days—Civil War
Printed for private use.
New York—D. Van Nostrand, 1870.

Hoyt, John W.
Reply to Charles W. Eliot's address in opposition to a National University, 1873.

Hudson River Traveler's Guide
New York—Gaylord Watson, 1871.

Hutchinson, Thomas
The witchcraft delusion of 1692 . . . from an unpublished manuscript (an early draft of his history of Massachusetts) in the Massachusetts archives. With notes by William Frederick Poole.
Boston—Privately printed, 1870.

Illinois—Organic Laws
Springfield, 1871.

Indian Campaigns—1779

The order book of Capt. Leonard Bleeker, Major of Brigade in the early part of the expedition under Gen. James Clinton, against the Indian settlements of western New York.
New York—Joseph Sabin, 1865.

Indian Question

About two hundred pamphlets dealing with the problem during the Hayes administration and later; some studies of individual tribes.

Indian Rights and Our Duties

An address delivered at Amherst, Hartford, etc., by Heman Humphreys, 1829.
Amherst—1830.

Indians—Civilization of

The reign of felicity, being a plan for civilizing the Indians of North America; without infringing on their national or individual independence. In a coffee-house dialogue, between a courtier, an esquire, a clergyman and a farmer.
London—T. Spence, 1796.

Indians—Eastern

Instructions for treating with the Eastern Indians given to the Commissioners . . . by the Hon. Spencer Phips, 1752.
Boston—1865.

Indians—North American

Remarks on the Indians of North America in a letter to an Edinburgh Reviewer.
'Philadelphus.'
London — Thomas and George Underwood, 1822.

Indians—Pequot War

Reprint of the History of John Mason—1637.
Edited by Thomas Prince, 1736.
New York—J. Sabin & Sons, 1869.

Ireland, James

The life of James Ireland who was, for many years, pastor of the Baptist Church . . . in Frederick and Shenandoah Counties, Virginia.
Winchester, Pa.—J. Foster, 1819.

Jackson, Andrew

re: Candidacy. Hints to Pennsylvania Democrats.
Anonymous.
August 25, 1826.

James, William

Warden refuted: being a Defense of the British Navy against the misrepresentations of a work recently published at Edinburgh . . . by D. B. Warden, late consul for the United States at Paris, etc., etc., in a letter to the Author of that work.
London—J. M. Richardson, 1819.

James River and Kanaroha Canal

Memorial to the National Board of Trade, March, 1870.

Janes, Thomas P.

A manual of Georgia for the use of immigrants and capitalists.
Atlanta—1878.

Janin, Jules

The American in Paris during the Winter.
New York—Burgess Stringer, 1844.

Jefferson, Thomas: Notes on Virginia

Observations on Mr. Jefferson's Notes on Virginia which appear to have a tendency to subvert religion, and establish a false philosophy.
New York—1804.

Johnson, Bradley T.

Report on the public debt of Virginia. ·
Richmond—James E. Goode, 1878.

Johnson, Edwin F.

Report to the Board of Directors of the Northern Pacific Railroad—1869.

Jones, Charles C.

Siege of Savannah in December, 1864, and the Confederate operations in Georgia.
Albany—Joel Munsell, 1874.

Jones, Maurice C.

A red rose from the olden time; or a ramble through the annals of the Rose Inn, on the Barony of Nazareth, in the days of the province: based on "The Old Inns at Nazareth." A paper read at the centenary of the "Nazareth Inn," June 9, 1871.
Philadelphia—King and Baird, 1872.

Josh Billings' Almanac for the Year of our Lord, 1873

New York—G. W. Carleton & Co., 1873.

Kelley, William D.

Letter to the citizens of the fourth congressional district of Pennsylvania.
Philadelphia—H. C. Baird & Co., 1875.

Kellogg, Robert H.
Life and death in rebel prisons.
Hartford, Conn.—L. Stebbins, 1865.

Kwang Chang Ling
Why should the Chinese go?
San Francisco—Bruce's Book and Job Printing House, 1878.

Lafayette, Marquis de
Outlines of the principal events in the life of—
By G. Ticknor.
Old note in the volume says that this article was submitted to Lafayette for his approval.
Boston—Cummings Hilliard & Co., 1825.

Lake Superior Improvement Convention
The great northern waterway. Report of the proceedings of the convention.
St. Paul, Minn.—Pioneer Press, 1879.

Lang, William W.
Relative increase of population and production; Commercial relations of the United States with Mexico, China, Japan, South America, and the Pacific Islands; The Southwestern system of railroads—Its value and national importance, 1881.

Lang, William W.
Texas and her capabilities, 1881.

Lanman, Charles
The Private Life of Daniel Webster.
New York—Harper & Bros., 1852.

Latrobe, J. H. B.
Chickasaw Claim to four square miles in the Big Sandy under the Treaty of June 22, 1852.
1869.

Latrobe, J. H. B.
The first steamboat voyage on the Western waters.
Baltimore, 1871.

Latrobe, J. H. B.
A lost chapter in the history of the steamboat.
Baltimore, 1871.

(Lee, Arthur)
A second appeal to the justice and interests of the people, on the measures respecting America—by the Author of the first.
London—J. Almon, 1775.

Legal Tender Act
Extra sheets from Spaulding's History of legal tender paper money issued during the great rebellion. Legal Tender Act. . . . Second Edition.
Buffalo, N. Y.—Baker, Jones & Co., 1875.

Legal Tender Act
Opinions delivered by the Judges of the Court of Appeals on the constitutionality of the Act of Congress, declaring treasury notes a legal tender for the payment of debts.
Albany, N. Y.—Weed, Parsons & Co., 1863.

Lewis, Winslow
Addresses—New England Historic Genealogical Society.
1862-1866.

Lexington and Fayette County, (Ky.)
Auxiliary Colonization Society.
Second annual report of the managers. . . . July 8, 1828.
Lexington, Ky. — Smith and Palmer, 1828.

Lincoln, Abraham
An address by George Putnam before the citizens of Roxbury on the occasion of the death of Lincoln.
Roxbury—Weston, 1865.

Lincoln, Abraham
Address by Andrew L. Stone, Park Church, Boston.
Boston—300 copies printed for J. K. Wiggin, 1865.

Lincoln, Abraham
Celebration by the Colored People's Educational Monument Association in Memory of Lincoln, July 4, 1865.
Washington—McGill & Withrow, 1865.

Lincoln, Abraham
Funeral sermon by Richard B. Duane.
Providence, R. I.—H. H. Thomas & Co., 1865.

Lincoln, Abraham
"The Heroic Succession" — oration by August J. H. Duganne, Cooper Institute, April 15, 1867.
German Radical Republican Central Committee.

Lincoln, Abraham
Personal Reminiscences of Lincoln.
New York—Scribner's, 1878.

Lincoln, Abraham
Proceedings of the city council of Providence on the death of Abraham Lincoln. . . . Oration by William Binney.
Providence, R. I.—Knowles, Anthony & Co., 1865.

Litchfield, Connecticut.
Centennial Celebration.
Hartford—E. Hunt, 1851.

Litchfield (Conn.) Female Academy
Chronicles of a Pioneer School, 1792-1833.

Livingston, John (Josiah Deadhead)
Analysis of the Erie Reorganization Bill, 1879.

Livingston, John
New Chapters of Erie.
New York—1876.

Livingston, John
The perils of the nation—bribery, dishonesty, usurpations and despotism of the railway corporations.
Address before the Workingmen's and Farmers' Union, 1877.

Lockwood, Ingersoll
Sammy and Burchy at the Union School.
(Hayes—Tilden).
New York—1876.

Lord, Eleazar
Six letters on the necessity and practicability of a national currency and the principles and measures essential thereto.
New York — Anson D. F. Randolph, 1862.

Louisiana Elections
Contemporary pamphlets.
1876-1881.

Lynch, John A. (John A. Than)
The Atlantic and Great Western Canal.
Washington—McGill & Witherow, 1873.

Lynch, John A.
A letter to the People of the United States on the present condition of public affairs.
Washington, 1872.

Machias, Maine
Centennial Anniversary of Settlement, 1863.

MacKenzie, William L.
The life and times of Martin Van Buren.
Boston—Cooke & Co., 1846.

Maine, State of
5th Annual Report of the Maine Board of Agriculture.
Augusta—State Printer, 1860.

Manitoba and the Canadian Northwest—1877
Also revised edition, 1879.

Mansfield (Lord)
The plea of the Colonies, on the charges brought against them by Lord Mansfield and others, in a letter to his Lordship.
London—J. Almon, 1776.

Manypenny, George W.
Commissioner of Indian Affairs.
Letter to Thomas H. Benton, May 21, 1855.

Marshall, James
The nation's prospects of peace. A discourse.
Philadelphia—King and Baird, 1864.

Marstons of Salem (The)
Memoirs of the three Benjamin Marstons with a brief genealogy of some of their descendants.
By John L. Watson, 1873.

Martyrs' Monument Association
Martyrs to the Revolution in the British Prison Ships in the Wallabout Bay.
New York—W. H. Arthur, 1855.

Maryland Historical Society
Addresses and Reports.
1844, 1850, 1854, 1858, 1866, 1867, 1868.

Mason, John
Capt. John Mason, the founder of New Hampshire . . . together with a memoir by Charles Wesley Tuttle.
Edited by John Ward Dean.
Edition of 250 copies.
Boston—Prince Society, 1887.

Massachusetts Banking System
Bank bills or paper currency, and the banking system. of Massachusetts.
By a Conservative.
Boston—Little, Brown & Co., 1856.

Massachusetts Governors
Valedictory address to the legislature.
By John A. Andrew.
January 4, 1866.

Massachusetts Historical Society
Catalogue of the books, pamphlets, newspapers, maps, charts, manuscripts, etc., in the library of the Massachusetts Historical Society.
Boston—John Eliot, 1811.

Maverick, Samuel
A briefe description of New England and the severall townes therein together

with the present government thereof—
1660.
Reprinted from a manuscript in the
British Museum, 1885.

Menecier, C.
Le Credit Mobile ou la Richesse par le
Travail et L'Extinction des Emprints
et des Impots.
Marseilles, France—J. Doucet, 1877 and
1879.

Messinger Family Genealogy
Compiled by George W. Messinger.
Albany—Joel Munsell, 1863.

Methodist Episcopal Church
About one hundred pamphlets, 1870
1890.

Mexico—Frontier Troubles
Report of the permanent committee ap-
pointed at a meeting of the citizens of
Brownsville, Texas.
Brownsville—J. S. Mansur, 1875.

Miami University — Union Literary
Society
Address to the Members on Responsi-
bilities of Men of Genius.
By A. Campbell.
Bethany, Va.—A Campbell, 1844.
(For other material see Ohio Imprints)

Michelet, M.
History of France, from the earliest
period to the present time, 4 vols.
New York—D. Appleton & Co., 1845.

Michigan—Admission to the Union
Journal of the proceedings of the convention of delegates chosen by electors
. . . for the purpose of taking into
consideration the proposition of Congress relating to the admission of the
State of Michigan into the Union.
Pontiac, Mich.—S. N. Gantt, 1836.

Micmac Indians
An account of the Aborigines of Nova
Scotia, called the Micmac Indians.
London—Luke Hansard & Sons, 1822.

Military Order of the Loyal Legion
Several hundred pamphlets.

Minneapolis and St. Anthony Tribune's Annual Exhibit of the
Manufacturing and commercial industry,
1871.

Minnesota—Advantage to Settlers
1868 and 1869.
Published by the State.

Minnesota Editorial Association
Annual meetings 1867-1870.

Minnesota Historical Society
Annals 1850, 1851, 1853.

Minnesota Historical Society
Annual reports 1868-1871, 1873.

Minnesota Historical Society
Charter, constitution, by-laws.
St. Paul—Remaley & Hall, 1868.

Minnesota Historical Society
Collections 1864, 1867, 1870.

Minnesota: Its Resources and Progress
Minneapolis—Tribune, 1872.

Minnesota Old Settlers Association
A sketch of the organization, objects and
membership.
St. Paul—1872.

Missionary Tour West of the Alle-
ghany Mountains
Report of a missionary tour west of the
Alleghany Mountains, performed
under the direction of the Massachu-
setts Missionary Society.
By Samuel J. Mills and Daniel Smith.
Andover, Mass.—Flagg & Gould, 1815.

Mississippi Company
A full and impartial account of the Com-
pany of Mississippi . . . projected and
settled by M. Law. In French and
English.
London—R. Francklin, 1720.

Mississippi (and Ohio) River
Towns. Pages 11-128 inclusive only. No
cover or date.

Mississippi River Improvement
The commerce and navigation of the
valley of the Mississippi; and also that
appertaining to the city of St. Louis:
considered, with reference to the improvement by the general government
of the Mississippi River and its principal tributaries; being a report prepared by authority of the delegates
from the city of St. Louis, for the use
of the Chicago convention of July 5,
1847.
St. Louis, Mo.—Chambers & Knapp.

Mississippi River Improvement Con-
vention
Proceedings of the convention held at
Dubuque, Iowa.
Dubuque Daily Times Steam Book
Press, 1866.

Mississippi River Navigation
The speeches of Mr. Ross and Mr.
Morris, etc.
1803.

O'Callaghan, E. B.
Voyage of George Clarke, Esq. to America, with introduction and notes by E. B. O'Callaghan.
Edition—100 copies.
New York Colonial Tracts, no. II.
Albany—Joel Munsell, 1867.

Ohio, State of
Several hundred pamphlets, most of them reports.
State officers or boards, 1869-1890. A few earlier or later than these dates.

Ohio Geology Map
New York—J. H. Cotton & Co., 1856.

Oneida Community Mutual Criticism
Office of the American Socialist.
Oneida, N. Y., 1876.

Owen, A. K.
Austin—Topolovampa Pacific Survey for Commercial and Scientific Purposes.
1877.

Owen, A. K.
Great Southern Transoceanic & International Air Line, Asia to Europe, via Mexico and the Southern States.
Philadelphia—Rowley & Chew, 1873.

Packard, Stephen B.
Speech at the Republican mass meeting in ratification of the Republican National and State tickets.
New Orleans—Mechanics Institute, 1876.

Paine, Thomas
The American Crisis.
London—James Watson, 1835.

Palfrey, John Gorham
A discourse pronounced at Barnstable on the third of September, 1839, at the celebration of the second centennial anniversary of the settlement of Cape Cod.
Boston—Ferdinand Andrews, 1840.

Parsons, Theophilus
Slavery—its origin, influence and destiny. Second edition.
Boston—William Carter & Brother, 1863.

Parton, James
. . . General Butler in New Orleans; being a history of the administration of the department of the Gulf in the year 1862; with an account of the capture of New Orleans, and a sketch of the previous career of the General, civil and military. People's ed.
New York—Mason Brothers, 1864.

Parton, James
Life of John Jacob Astor.
New York—American News Co., 1865.

Peabody Education Fund
Reports and papers covering the years from 1870-1893.

Peabody Museum Reports
Covering the years 1868-1912.

Penn, William
A discourse delivered before the Society for the Commemoration of the Landing of William Penn, by C. J. Ingersoll.
Philadelphia—R. H. Small, 1825.

Penn, William
Journal of his travels in Holland and Germany in 1677. . . . Fourth edition.
London—Darton & Harvey, 1835.

Penn, William
Sketch of the Life and Character of William Penn.
Philadelphia — Association of Friends, Tract no. 73.

Pequot War
Reprint of the History of John Mason, 1637.
Edited by Thomas Prince, 1736.
Reprinted by J. Sabin & Sons.
New York, 1869.

Philadelphia—Military Map
1861-1865.

Philadelphia Public Ledger
Historical sketch.
July, 1870.

Phinney, Elias
History of the Battle of Lexington—April 19, 1775.
Boston—Phelps & Farnham, 1825.

Pierce, Franklin
Our New President.
In Putnam's Monthly, Sept., 1853.

Pitt, William
A letter to the Earl of Chatham on the Quebec Bill.
London—for T. Cadell, 1774.

Pittsburgh, Washington and Baltimore Railroad
Formal opening.
Baltimore—Sun Book Establishment, 1871.

Plumbe, John
Sketches of Iowa and Wisconsin taken

during a residence of three years in these territories.
St. Louis, Mo.—Chambers, Harris and Knapp, 1839.

Political Allegory
The diamond mirror, reflecting political points for the people, with a printed centennial.
By Paulus.
Philadelphia—1876.

Political Parties—Democrat
Hints to Pennsylvania Democrats.
August 25, 1826.

Political Parties—Union Republican
National Union Republican Conventions. Calls and platforms.
1856-1872.

Porter, Noah
An historical discourse delivered at the celebration of the 100th anniversary of the Congregational Church at Farmington, Conn.
Hartford, Conn. — Case, Lockwood and Brainard, 1873.

Power, J. C.
The Springfield annual for 1872. Devoted to manufactures and business in general. No. 2.
Springfield, Ill.—John H. Johnson, 1872.

Prentiss, George L.
Our national bane; or, the dry-rot in American politics. A tract ... touching civil service reform.
New York—Anson D. F. Randolph, 1877.

Presbyterian Church — Rockaway, N. J.
A brief history.
Newark, N. J.—Uzal J. Tuttle and Co., 1833.

Presbyterian Church — Rockaway, N. J.
Fortieth anniversary sermon.
New York—J. M. Sherwood, 1849.

Presbyterian Synod of Virginia
Prayer and consultation.
Proceedings of the meeting.
Richmond, Va.—William Macfarlane, 1838.

Presidential Candidates—1876
Biographical sketches.
A valuable book for the times. The lives of the Presidential Candidates.
New York—American Publishing and Manufacturing Co., 1876.

Preston Family Memoranda
Compiled by John Mason Brown.
Frankfort, Ky., 1870.

Preuss, H. Clay
Columbus Crockett to General Grant on the Indian Policy. (Poem).
Washington—J. Bradley Adams, 1873.

Price, Richard
Additional observations on the nature and value of civil liberty, and the war with America: also observations on schemes for raising money by public loans; an historical deduction and analysis of the national debt; and a brief account of the debts and resources of France.
Second edition.
London—T. Cadell, 1777.

Price, Richard
Experience preferable to theory. An answer to Dr. Price's observation on the nature of civil liberty, and the justice and policy of the war with America.
London—T. Payne, 1776.

Price, Richard
Observations on the nature of civil liberty, the principles of government, and the justice and policy of the war with America. To which is added an appendix containing a statement of the national debt.
London—T. Cadell, 1776.

Prince Society (The)
Organized 1858 ... incorporated 1874.

Prisons and Prison Reform
About one hundred pamphlets, most of them dated 1880-1893.

Pulteney, William
Thoughts on the present state of affairs with America, and the means of conciliation.
The fourth edition.
London—J. Dodsley & T. Cadell, 1778.

Quebec, Siege of 1759
Extract from a manuscript Journal ... kept by Colonel Malcolm Fraser, then Lieutenant of the 78th (Fraser's Highlanders) and serving in that campaign.

Quebec Literary and Historical Society

Railroads
Several hundred pamphlets and reports, most of them for the years 1870-1890.
See also Land Grants.

Ramson, Rawson W.
Report of the Bahamas for the year 1864.
London—G. E. Eyre, 1866.

Reavis, L. W.
Facts and arguments in favor of the removal of the National Capital to the Mississippi Valley.
St. Louis, Mo.—Democrat, 1870.

Rees, James
The dramatic authors in America.
Philadelphia—G. B. Zieber & Co., 1845.

Reichel, W. C.
Names which the Lenni Lennape or Delaware Indians gave to rivers, streams and localities. . . . Prepared from manuscript by John Heckewelder.
Bethlehem, Pa.—H. T. Clauder, 1872.

Religion
Several hundred pamphlets, comprising sermons, tracts, history of churches, sects, etc. The material on the Methodist Episcopal Church and its activities is especially complete.

Religious Sects—Associate Reformed Synod
Extracts from the minutes of the acts and proceedings of the Associate Reformed Synod with an appendix, containing the substance of Dr. Horne's preface to his commentary on the Psalms; and an extract from the Christian Remembrancer.
New York—S. Loudon & Son, 1793.

Religious Sects—Episcopal
Memoirs of Ammi Rogers, etc.
Tenth edition.
Watertown, N. Y.—Knowlton and Rice, 1844.

Religious Sects—Presbyterian
Biographical Memoirs of the late Rev. John Gano of Frankfort, Ky.
New York — Southwick & Hardcastle, 1806.

Religious Sects—Presbyterian
Historical sketch of the Synod of New Jersey.
Ravand K. Rodgers.
New Brunswick, N. J.—Terhune and Van Anglon, 1861.

Republican Party
Pamphlets especially of the period 1872-1882.

Reorganized Republic (The)
By a citizen.
Reprinted from the Radical.
Virginia City, Nevada, 1871.

Report of a French Protestant Refugee, in Boston, 1687
Tr. from the French by E. T. Fisher.
Brooklyn, N. Y., 1868.

Revolutionary War—Battles
The Fight at Diamond Island, 1777.
B. F. De Costa.
New York—J. Sabin & Sons, 1872.

Revolutionary War—Officers
Memoir of Colonel John Allan with a Genealogy.
George H. Allan.
Albany, N. Y.—Joe Munsell, 1867.

Revolutionary War—Reminiscences
My ride to the barbecue, or, revolutionary reminiscences of the old Dominion.
By an ex-member of Congress.
New York—S. A. Rollo, 1860.

Revolutionary War—Societies
Martyrs' Monument Association.
New York—W. H. Arthur, 1855.

Richardson, D. M.
A plan for returning to specie payments without financial revulsion.
Detroit, Mich., 1869.

Richardson, D. M.
Policy of finance.
A plan for returning to specie payments and free banking.
Washington—Chronicle Print, 1874.

Riley, Josiah
Democracy—The First Century of the National Life.
Is Political Self-Government a Failure?
San Francisco—John H. Cormany & Co., 1876.

Robbins, E. Y.
The war in America: and what England, or the people of England, may do to restore peace.
New York—M. B. Bronn & Co., 1863.

(Robbins, Elliott)
Panacea for the healing of the nation.
Centennial of the foundation of the government of the United States.
New York—Globe Stationery, 1876.

Roberts, Edward P.
Health ordinances of the corporation of

the city of Baltimore, to which is pre-
fixed and index, compiled and prepared by the Board of Health.
Baltimore—William Ogden Niles, 1824.

Roberts, W. Milnor
Report of a Reconnaisance of the route
for the Northern Pacific Railroad between Lake Superior and Puget Sound
via the Columbia River, 1869.

Roelker, Bernard
Argument in favor of the Constitution-
ality of the Legal Tender Clause.
New York—F. W. Christern, 1863.

Root, James P.
(1) Who shall count the electoral votes
and declare the results?
(2) The power of Congress in regard to
the Presidential Election.
Chicago—Beach, Barnard & Co., 1876.

Ross, John
Letter from John Ross, the principal
chief of the Cherokee Nation, to a
gentleman of Philadelphia. 1837 (?).

Runkle, Ben P.
Address to the Freedmen of Kentucky.
Louisville, Ky.—Calvert, Tippett & Co.,
1868.

Sabine, Lorenzo
Speech on the death of Maj. Gen. James
Wolfe, September 13, 1859.
Hundredth anniversary.
Boston—A. Williams & Co., 1859.

St. Louis, Alton and Terre Haute
Railroad
Suit vs. Charles Butler, Samuel J. Til-
den, Russell Soge and Robert Bayard.
New York—K. Wells Sackett and Bro.,
1876.

St. Louis Guide Book
Strangers Guide in and about St. Louis.
1872.

St. Paul Chamber of Commerce
Reports.
1868-1869.

Sammy and Burchy at the Union
School
(Tilden and Hayes)
Ingersoll Lockwood
New York, 1876.

Sampson, Deborah
The Female Review.
Life of Deborah Sampson, the female
soldier in the war of the Revolution.

With introduction and notes by John
Adams Vinton.
Edition 250 copies, small Quarto—no.
68.
Boston—J. K. Wiggin, 1866.

Sampson, Marmaduke B.
Central America and the transit between
the oceans.
New York—S. W. Benedict, 1850.

San Diego (Calif.)
San Diego—the California terminus of
the Texas and Pacific Railroad, 1872.

San Francisco Board of Trade
Report on the Inter-Oceanic Canal.
"The Key of the Pacific."
San Francisco—Dempster Bros., 1880.

San Francisco Real Estate
Report on condition.
San Francisco—Evening Picayune, 1851.

Sands, Nathaniel
Letter to the Secretary of the Treasury
on taxation, finance and re-organization of the tariff.
New York—George F. Nesbit and Co.,
1869.

Scott, F. J.
Suggestions concerning a national cur-
rency, 1873.
Author's presentation copy.

Scott, Winfield
Life of—
Campaign literature, 1852.

Scovell's Farmers' and Mechanics'
Almanac
New York, 1870.

Segar, Joseph
Letter to Alexander Rives. Opinion of
the Republican Party by one who was
a member of the old Whig Party, 1876.

Sheppard, J. H.
Brief history of the New England His-
toric-Genealogical Society, 1862.

Siddons, (Muzafir)
Yankeeland in her trouble.
An Englishman's correspondence dur-
ing the war.
October, 1864.

Silver Question
About one hundred pamphlets, dating
from about 1876-1894.

Simms, William A.
South Carolina in the Revolutionary
War.
Charleston, S. C.—Walker and James,
1853.

Slater, William
Virginia: containing valuable information to those who think of emigrating there.
London—J. Kitto, 1872.

Slater Fund
Reports and publications during the years when President Hayes was a trustee—1882-1893.

Smith, Daniel (and Mills, S. J.)
Report of a missionary tour through that part of the United States which lies west of the Alleghany Mountains: performed under the direction of the Massachusetts Missionary Society.
Andover, Mass.—Flagg & Gould, 1815.

Songs—Hayes & Wheeler
Campaign—1876.
(1) Songs of the boys in blue.
New York Union Committee.
(2) State Campaign Song Book.
Melrose, Mass.—Campaign Song Co.
(3) Republican Campaign Song Book.
Cincinnati—F. W. Helmick.
(4) Rutherford B. Hayes Songs
T. K. Preuss.

South—Political Situation
Article from the New Orleans Bee of August 20, 1871, on the political situation. By R. Hutcheson.
New Orleans — Pelican Book and Job Printing, 1871.

South America—Report on the West Coast of—
Associated Industries of the United States, 1878 (?).

Southern Policy—Hayes
About fifty pamphlets, 1877-1879.

Southern Question
The Bourbon conspiracy to rule or destroy the nation.
By a Georgia Republican.
Washington—Republic Publishing Co., 1875.

Southern States — Economic. Conditions
The cotton states in the spring and summer of 1875.
New York—D. Appleton, 1876.

Southern Transcontinental Railway Line
National railroad convention proceedings, 1875.

St. Louis, Mo.—Woodward, Tiernan & Hale, 1875.

Spain—Cuban Relations
The Geneva pamphlet.
New York—D. Appleton & Co., 1876.

Sparks, Jared
Remarks on a "Reprint of the original letters from Washington to Joseph Reed, during the American Revolution, referred to in the pamphlets of Lord Mahon and Mr. Sparks.
Boston—Little, Brown & Co., 1853.

Spaulding, Elbridge Gerry
One hundred years of Progress in the business of banking, 1876.

Speer, William
The lessons of 1860.
A discourse delivered before the Young Men's Christian Association of St. Paul.
St. Paul Press Printing Co., 1861.

Squier, E. G.
Honduras Interoceanic Railway.
Preliminary report.
New York—Tubbs, Nesmuth and Teall, 1854.

Squier, E. G.
Observations on the uses of the mounds of the West, with an attempt at their classification.
New Haven, R. I.—B. L. Hamlen, 1847.

Stamp Act
Correct copies of the two protests against the bill to repeal the American Stamp Act of last session.
With lists of the speakers and voters.
Paris—Chez J. W. Imprimeur, 1766.

Starr, M. B.
The coming struggle; or what the people on the Pacific Coast think of the coolie invasion.
San Francisco—Excelsior Office, 1873.

Steamboat History
The first steamboat voyage on the western waters.
Baltimore, 1871.

Stewart, J. A.
Conservative views.
The government of the United States: What is it? Comprising a correspondence with A. H. Stephens. . . .
Atlanta, Ga.—Phillips & Crew, 1869.

Stuart, James F.
Three pamphlets on the California land frauds of 1872.

Suffrage—Negro
Argument in favor of the constitutionality of the franchise law, before the Supreme Court of Tennessee.
Nashville—Press and Times, 1867.

Swallow, G. C.
Geological report of the country along the line of the Southwestern branch of the Pacific Railroad, States of Missouri.
St. Louis—George Knapp, 1859.

Tariff—Protective
About fifty pamphlets, 1876-1890.

Taylor, Frank H.
Random notes from the Diary of a Man in Search of the West through St. Paul and Minneapolis in 1881.

Taylor, James W.
The Sioux War: What shall we do with it?
The Sioux Indians: What shall we do with them?
St. Paul—Press Printing Co., 1862.

Tebault, C. H.
New Orleans: what she owes and what she does not owe.
New Orleans—Franklin House, 1877.

Temperance Question
About fifty pamphlets, most of them from the years 1876-1890.

Texas—Description
Facts relating to northeastern Texas. Condensed from notes made during a tour through that portion of the United States for the purpose of examining the country as a field for emigration.
London—Simpkin, Marshall & Co., 1849.

Texas—Resources, Etc.
Texas, her resources and capabilities—being a description of the state and the inducements she offers to those seeking homes in a new country.
Austin—E. D. Slater, 1881.

Texas Almanac for 1859
Galveston News also for 1860, 1861, 1867.

Thackeray, William Makepeace (Titmarsh, Michael Angelo)
Notes of a journey from Cornhill to Cairo.
New York—Wiley & Putnam, 1846.

Thompson, J.
Reflections on the destructive consequences of the erroneous financial measures of the government in the past twelve years and suggestions for future action to repair the mischief.
New York—Charles Vogt, 1877.

Tiffany, Osmond
A sketch of the life and services of Gen. Otho Holland Williams.
Baltimore—John Murphy & Co., 1851.

Tilden, Samuel J.
Twelve pamphlets, most of them dated 1876.

Tobey, Edward S.
American shipping interests: their revival a national necessity.
Boston Board of Trade, 1871.
Boston—Daily Advertiser Press

Tucker, Josiah
A letter to Edmund Burke, Esq.; member of Parliament for the city of Bristol and agent for the colony of New York, etc. . . .
Second edition corrected.
Gloucester—R. Raikes, 1775.

Tucker, Josiah
A series of answers to certain popular objections against separating from the Rebellious Colonies and discarding them entirely, being the concluding tract of the Dean of Gloucester on the subject of American affairs.
Gloucester—R. Raikes, 1776.

Tucker, Josiah
Tract V. The respective pleas and arguments of the mother country, and of the colonies, distinctly set forth; and the impossibility of a compromise of differences, or a mutual concession of rights, plainly demonstrated. With a prefatory epistle to the plenipotentiaries of the late Congress at Philadelphia.
Gloucester—R. Raikes, 1775.

Ullman, Daniel
Organization of colored troops and the regeneration of the South.
February 5, 1867.
Washington—Great Republic Office, 1868.

United States Government
Between three and four hundred pamphlets covering records of departments and officials, many of them for the years of the Hayes Administration, 1877-1881.

tah—Resources and Attractions, 1879
Utah Board of Trade.

erplanck, Gulian C.
Discourse before the New York Historical Society, December 7, 1818.
New York—James Eastburn & Co., 1818.

irginia — Commercial Agents Report, 1864

irginia—Fourteenth Regiment
Proceedings relative to the existing war, January 24, 1865.

irginia Bible Society
Address ·of the managers of the Bible Society of Virginia to the public.
Richmond—Samuel Pleasants, 1814.

ar of 1812
Muster roll of citizen soldiers at North Point and Fort McHenry, September 12 and 13, 1814.
Freeman & Goodsmith.
Baltimore—James Young, Printer.

arden Refuted
Being a defense of the British Navy against the misrepresentations of a work recently published at Edinburgh . . . by D. B. Warden, late Consul of the U. S. at Paris, etc., etc. . . .
In a letter to the author of that work by William James.
London—J. M. Richardson, 1819.

Warren, G. K.
Preliminary report of explorations in Nebraska and Dakota in the years 1855-1857.
Washington—Government Printing Office, 1875.

Webb and Shailer's Family School
Catalog of pupils.

(This was the school attended by President Hayes).
Middletown, Conn., 1841.

Webster, Daniel
An address delivered at the laying of the corner-stone of the Bunker Hill Monument.
Boston — Cummings, Hilliard & Co., 1825.

Webster, Daniel
A discourse delivered at Plymouth, December 22, 1820. In commemoration of the first settlement of New England.
Boston—Wells and Lilly, 1821.

Welles, Gideon
Lincoln and Seward: Views as to the relative position of the late President and Secretary of State.
New York—Sheldon and Company, 1874.

Williamson, M. T.
"Line of Policy" suggested for the Payment of the State Debt of Tennessee.
Memphis—Price, Jones & Co., 1876.

Wines, E. C.
International congress on the prevention and repression of crimes, including penal and reformatory treatment. Statement of the objects and results of negotiations with various continental governments in relation thereto. With the proceedings of a meeting held in London.
London, 1871.

Wood, John W.
Union and Secession in Mississippi.
Memphis — Saunders, Parrish & Whitmore, 1863.

Wright, George Frederick
About two hundred pamphlets by him on archaeology, geology and theology.

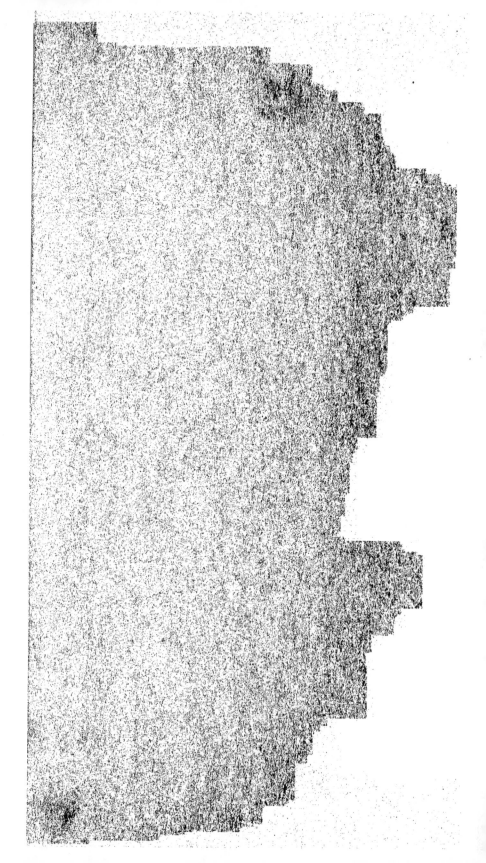

An Index and List

of the

LETTERS and PAPERS

of

Rutherford Birchard Hayes

Nineteenth President of the United States

WITH NOTES ON OTHER SOURCE MATERIAL
AT THE HAYES MEMORIAL LIBRARY,
SPIEGEL GROVE STATE PARK,
FREMONT, OHIO

Published by
Ohio State Archaeological and Historical Society
Columbus, Ohio

An Index and List

of the

LETTERS and PAPERS

of

Rutherford Birchard Hayes
Nineteenth President of the United States

WITH NOTES ON OTHER SOURCE MATERIAL
AT THE HAYES MEMORIAL LIBRARY,
SPIEGEL GROVE STATE PARK,
FREMONT, OHIO

Published by
Ohio State Archaeological and Historical Society
Columbus, Ohio

INTRODUCTION

The Hayes Memorial Library at Fremont, Ohio, is the property of the State of Ohio by deed of gift to the State from Colonel Webb C. Hayes, son of President Rutherford B. Hayes. It is controlled and managed for the State by The Ohio State Archaeological & Historical Society which has its headquarters in Columbus, Ohio.

The Rutherford B. Hayes and Lucy Webb Hayes Foundation is an independent, privately endowed Association formed to perpetuate the name and fame of Rutherford B. Hayes and his wife, Lucy Webb Hayes. The Foundation is, in part, furthering the purposes for which it was formed by assisting The Hayes Memorial Library to place its material and facilities at the service of competent historical scholars and research workers. It plans to aid in the development and enlargement of the original and secondary source material in the Hayes Memorial Library, particularly with respect to the Reconstruction Period in American history, and hopes that ultimately the Memorial Library will become one of the important centers of source material covering that period.

The Life of Rutherford Birchard Hayes, by Charles Richard Williams, was published in two volumes by Houghton Mifflin Company in 1914. This edition was followed by a new edition published by The Ohio State Archaeological & Historical Society. *The Diary and Letters of Rutherford Birchard Hayes*, edited by Charles Richard Williams, was published in five volumes by The Ohio State Archaeological & Historical Society between 1922 and 1926. That Society also published an *Illustrated Catalogue of Spiegel Grove State Park, The Hayes Memorial Library and Museum, and the Hayes Homestead* in 1926. At the time these volumes were published the huge mass of Hayes manuscripts was totally unorganized. It was not only unindexed but was in greater part unfiled and unassembled. Mr. Williams spent untold hours of the most painstaking labor in finding and assembling the material from which his works above mentioned were prepared and edited.

The Board of Trustees of the Hayes Foundation secured the services of Miss Ruth M. Boring of the Remington Rand, Inc., to arrange, file, and index the mass of Hayes papers in the Hayes Memorial Library to make them easily available to research scholars. A portion of the admirable work done by Miss Boring is shown by the accompanying Index and List which gives some idea of the organized material now available for use. The mass of the material is so great that it would take years to prepare a complete calendar of it. The Index simply mentions the most important events, subjects, and personages with which the material deals. Fuller information on any topic or topics may be secured by communicating with The Hayes Memorial Library at Fremont.

THE HAYES MEMORIAL CONTAINS THE FOLLOWING TYPES OF SOURCE MATERIAL OF INTEREST TO STUDENTS OF THE HAYES PERIOD:

1. Books:
   - (a) Americana collected by Rutherford B. Hayes, including the Robert Clarke collection which he bought from this collector and dealer.
   - (b) Literature, embracing some presentation copies and first editions of American authors.
   - (c) Government publications, both state and national.
   - (d) Works on the Hayes period. This collection is growing rapidly, as it is the field in which the Library is to specialize.

2. Pamphlets—between 9000 and 10,000.

   While there are some old pamphlets of the 17th and 18th century among them, the larger portion are of the Hayes period or just preceding it. This material is not classified.

3. Hayes Letters and Papers:
   - (a) Correspondence of Lucy Webb Hayes.
   - (b) Hayes Family Correspondence. This is entirely personal and social in character.
   - (c) Invitations and Programs. No correspondence, but gives some interesting light on the social customs of the period, as well as the many calls on the president and his family.
   - (d) Hayes File:
     - (1) Letters to Rutherford B. Hayes.
     - (2) Letters by Rutherford B. Hayes. These letters are filed in the Hayes section and not with the material of the correspondents, partly because it is extremely fragmentary, and partly because it may eventually be made a file by itself. The fragmentary character is due to the fact that carbon copies were not in use, and relatively few letters have been given up by their recipients. A number of drafts of letters are included.

4. Hayes Diary:

   This covers all the years from his school days to a few weeks before his death in January of 1893. It forms the basis of the *Life and Diary* by Mr. Williams.

5. Newspaper Clippings:

   Covering the Administration years. There are 127 volumes, covering social life as well as the various political issues of importance. It is partially indexed.

6. Letter Books:

   There are fifteen volumes containing drafts of letters received during the presidential period. The arrangement is chronological.
   There are three letter-press books covering a part of the governorship period. These are impresses of the letters themselves.

The contents of the Hayes letters and papers have been carefully indexed by subject, and the material itself filed for easy reference by research students.

In order to give some conception of the character and variety of the material, the following lists of subjects and names are given. The list of subjects indicates only main issues selected from an index of 22,000 cards. The lists of names represent about one percent of those in the file, and were chosen partly because of the prominence of the correspondents and partly because of the amount and interest of the material.

A. Subject Index: Hayes Letters and
    Papers
    (Main divisions of a 22,000 card index)
Abolitionists
Abstinence
Adelbert College
Administration
    Articles
    Endorsement
    History of
    Results
    Suggestions
Agricultural Associations
Agriculture
    Advancement
    Department of
    Statistics
Alabama
Alaska
Albany, City of
Amendments—Constitutional
American Alliance
Anderson, Thomas C.
Annapolis Naval Academy
Anti-Saloon Movement
Anti-Slavery Movement
Applications
    (Listed Alphabetically)
Appointments
    (Listed Alphabetically)
Appointments
    Approval
    Confirmation
    Declined
    Objections
    Ohio State
    Protests

    Reports
    Withdrawals
Appropriation Bills
Arbitration
Argentine Republic
Arizona
Arkansas
Army
    Administration
    Appointments
    Bills
    Court Martials
    Dismissals
    Promotions
    Reunions
    Surgeons
Army of West Virginia
Arthur, Chester A.
Articles—Requests of Rutherford B.
    Hayes
Artists
Associations
Autograph
    Collections
    Requests for
Back Pay Grab
Backus Family
Bahamas (The)
Ballot
    Boxes
    Protection
    Qualifications
    Stuffing
Baltimore American (The)
Baltimore and Ohio Railroad
    Company

Maine
Maps
Maryland
Massachusetts
Medill, Joseph
Messages—Presidential
Methodist Episcopal Church
Mexican Affairs
Military Order of the Loyal Legion
Commandery-in-Chief
Commandery: State
Minnesota
Mississippi
Mississippi River Commission
Missouri
Mohonk Conference
Montana
Monuments and Men
Mormonism
Morton, Levi P.
Morton, Oliver P.
Morton, Oliver T.
Muskogee Nation
see also Indians
Nashville, City of
National Agricultural Association
National Civil Service Reform
League
National Homes for Soldiers and
Sailors
National Immigration Bureau
National Prison Congresses
Naval Academy
see Annapolis
Navy Department
Negroes
see also under Colored Race
Southern Situation
Education
Nevada
New England
New Hampshire
New Jersey
New Mexico
New Orleans
see also Louisiana
New York, City of

New York, State of
Campaign
Conventions
Governors
Political Situation
Nicholls, Francis T.
. see also Louisiana
Nomination
Letter of
Acceptance
North Carolina
Northern Pacific Railway
Noyes, Edward F.
Oberlin College
Office Holders
Appointments
Complaints
Dismissals
Dismissals for Cause
Re-appointments
Removals
Renewals
Rules covering
Office Seekers
(Listed Alphabetically)
Oglesby, Richard J.
Ohio, State of
Board of Charities
Centennials
Elections
General Assembly
Geological Survey
History
Institutions
Legislative Expense
National Guard
Republican Committee
Republican League
Society
Soldiers Orphans Home
Supreme Court
University
Ohio State Archaeological and
Historical Society
Ohio Wesleyan University
Oklahoma
Omaha Scandal
Ordinance of 1787
Oregon
Page, Walter H.
Pamphlets
(see note in list of source material)
Pan-American Congress

[11]

West Point Military Academy
   Applications
   Board of Visitors
   Re-organization
West Virginia
Western Lands
Western Reserve University
Wheeler, William A.
White, Andrew D.
White House
Willard, Frances E.
Windom, William

Winthrop, Robert
Wisconsin
Woman's Home Missionary Society
Womans Relief Corps
Womans Suffrage
Women's Christian Temperance Union
Wyoming
Yale College
Yates, Richard
Yellowstone Park
Yorktown Centennial

LIST OF IMPORTANT NAMES IN HAYES LETTERS AND PAPERS

Abbott, Edward J.
Abbott, Lyman
Abell, Benjamin L.
Abraham, James
Acklen, J. H.
Adams, C. F. (Jr.)
Adams Express Company
Ainger, D. B.
Ainsworth, George J.
Alabama Claims
Albany, City of
Albright, Charles
Alcorn, James L.
Alderman, E. R.
Aldis, A. O.
Aldrich, H. N.
Aldrich, L. F.
Alexander, A. J.
Alexander, J. W.
Allen, C. L.
Allen, Ethan A.
Allen, Frederick D.
Allen, George W.
Allen, H. N.
Allen, Robert (Jr.)
Allen, Stephen M.
Allen, Walter
Allison, W. B.
Allison, W. R.
Alloway, N. E.
Ambler, J. A.
American Alliance
American and British Claims
American Association for the Advancement
   of Science

American Economic Association
American Exchange in Europe
American Historical Association
American Iron and Steel Association
American Legion
American Missionary Association
Ames, Florian Winfield
Ammen, Daniel
Ampt, William M.
Anderson, Edward
Anderson, George H.
Anderson, H. O.
Anderson, Larz
Anderson, R. C.
Anderson, Samuel C.
Anderson, Thomas C.
Andersonville Survivors Association
Andrews, E. F.
Andrews, Emma S.
Andrews, J. W.
Andrews, John W.
Andrews, Marti n
Angell, James B.
Ansley, John
Anthony George F.
Anthony, H. B.
Anthony, Susan B.
Appleman, A. R.
Appleton D. & Company
Archer, R. L.
Arizona, Territory of
Arkansas, State of
Armstrong, Robert B.
Armstrong, Robert C.
Armstrong, W. W.

Arnold, George
Arthur, E. C.
Ashenhurst, John J.
Aston, Isaac C.
Astor, J. J.
Astor, William
Atkins, James
Austin, Emily L.
Austin, Henry
Austin, Horace
Austin, J. B.
Axtell, J. S.
Ayres, S. C.

Babbitt, Henry S.
Babcock, Benjamin F.
Babcock, O. E.
Bacon, John M.
Bacon, Leonard W.
Bacon, W. D.
Badeau, Adam
Badger, A. S.
Bagley, John J.
Bagwell, John D.
Bailey, Austin
Bailey, William L.
Baird, Chambers
Baird, Spencer F.
Baker, Conrad
Baker, Fred
Baker, George H.
Baker, L. N.
Baker, W. J.
Baker, William
Baker, William Emerson
Baker, William T.
Balch, Benjamin
Baldwin, C. C.
Baldwin, H. P.
Ball, George H.
Ballantine, William G.
Ballou, O. H.
Baltimore, City of
Baltimore and Ohio Railroad
Bancroft, George
Banks, N. P.
Bannerman, T. R.
Baptist Ministers
Barber, E. L.
Barber, J. Jay
Barber, S.
Barbour, Lucian
Bardeen, E. R.
Barholdt. Charles C.
Barker, Wharton
Barnes, Demas
Barnes, James W.
Barnes, Milton
Barnes, W. C.

Barnett, James
Barney, B. B.
Barney, J. K. (Mrs.)
Barr, Thomas F.
Barrett, Joseph E.
Barrett, Joseph H.
Barrow, Bright G.
Barrows, Elliott T.
Barrows, Isabel C.
Barrows, W. E.
Bartlett, J. P.
Bartlett, John R.
Bartley, T. W.
Barton, Clara
Bascom, W. T.
Bassett, Samuel
Bateman, Warner H.
Bates, G. H.
Bates, George C.
Bates, J. H.
Bates, James L.
Bauer, Seraph
Baxter, John
Bayard, Thomas F.
Bayne, Thomas M.
Bazell, James B.
Beach, G. Mason
Beach, Will G.
Bean, Theo. W.
Beard, A. W.
Beauregard, G. T.
Beck, James B.
Beckley, Alfred
Beckwith, George
Bedell, G. T.
Beebe, Eugene
Beecher, Henry Ward
Beelman, Charles S.
Beeson, John
Belcher, Edwin
Belknap, William W.
Bell, A.
Bell, D. V.
Bell, James H.
Bell, John W.
Belton, W. H.
Benedict Taft and Benedict
Benjamin, Charles F.
Bennett, James Gordon
Bennington Battle Monument Association
Benson, E. C.
Benson, Olaf
Bentley, John A.
Berea College
Bernard, Charles B.
Berwick, Edward
Bethune, James N.
Beveridge, John L.
Beyland, J. C. F.

Bickham, Thomas
Bickham, William D.
Bickham, Yeatman
Bicknell, Thomas W.
Biddle, George M.
Bierstadt, Albert
Bigelow, W. H.
Bingham, John A.
Binny, John R.
Birchard Library
Bird, Thomas W.
Birney, James
Bishop, J. P.
Bishop, Levi
Bishop, R. M.
Bit and Bridle Club
Black, A. M.
Black, John C.
Black, William C.
Blackburn, C: H.
Blackwell, H. B.
Blaine, James G.
Blair, Henry W.
Blair, J. H.
Blair Monument Association
Blake, Charles M.
Blake, James S.
Blake, John B.
Blanc, Albert
Bliss, Charles M.
Bliss, Eugene F.
Bliss, William H.
Bliven, C. E.
Blocker, O. H.
Blodget, Louis
Boardman, J. L.
Boardman, W. L.
Bodine, William B.
Bogardus, E.
Bohm, E. H.
Bok, Edward W.
Bolling, Robert
Bonaparte, Caroline
Bone, J. H. A.
Bone, James H.
Bonham, L. H.
Bonney, Charles C.
Bonte, J. H. C.
Booth, George A.
Booth, H. J.
Booth, John T,
Booth, Newton
Borden, Spencer
Boruch, M. D.
Bosley, S. Parker
Boston Board of Trade
Boston Journal
Boteler, A. R.
Botsford, James L.

Bourke, John G.
Bourne, Theodore
Boutcher, C. S.
Boutwell, George S.
Bovee, Marvin H.
Bowen, Clarence W.
Bowen, George S.
Bowen, Henry C.
Bowker, R. R.
Boyce, James P.
Boyd, Thomas
Boyle, James
Boynton, H. V.
Bradbury, Hannah B.
Bradford, A. W.
Bradford, Benjamin Rush
Bradford, Gamaliel
Bradlee, Caleb D.
Bradley, C. F.
Bradley, Joseph C.
Bradley, Joseph P.
Brady, James D.
Brady, Thomas J.
Brainerd, E. P.
Brainerd, John A.
Brand, Joseph C.
Brandeis, Louis D.
Branscombe, C. H.
Bray, J. F.
Brazee, John S.
Brearley, W. H.
Breckenridge, J. C.
Breslin, J. G.
Brewster, Benjamin Harris
Brewster, C. M. N.
Brewster, F. Carroll
Brice, A. G.
Brigden, Charles E.
Briggs, H. H.
Briggs, James A.
Briggs, L. Vernon
Brigham, J. H.
Brinck, P. C.
Brink, Edward R.
Brinkerhoff, Roeliff
Brinkerhoff, W. W.
Brinsmade, Allan T.
Bristow, B. H.
British and Foreign Anti-Slavery Society
Brockway, B.
Brockway, Z. R.
Brodhead, E. H.
Bronson, S. A.
Brooke, Francis M.
Brooke, Horace L.
Brooke, Hunter
Brooklyn Magazine (The)
Brooklyn Sunday School Union
Brooks, E. P.

Carabelli, Joseph
Carlile, John S.
Carlin, S.
Carlisle, J. G.
Carlisle, John
Carlisle Barracks
Carpenter, C. S.
Carpenter, L. Cass
Carpenter, Matt H.
Carr, E. A.
Carr, Gouverneur
Carrington, Henry B.
Carroll, Robert W.
Carson, E. T.
Carter, A. G. W.
Carter, George W.
Carter, John D.
Carter, Joseph F.
Carter, Robert
Cary, Samuel F.
Casanave, G.
Casey, Thomas Lincoln
Casner, Ellen D.
Cassaday, J. B.
Catholic Total Abstinence Union
Catley, H.
Cavender, John S.
Caznean, I. M.
Centennial Exposition 1876
Cessna, William K.
Chadbourne, P. A.
Chadwick, Daniel
Chaffee, J. B.
Chalfant, Edward J.
Chamberlain, A. E.
Chamberlain, D. H.
Chamberlain, Joshua L.
Chamberlain, W. I.
Chamberlain, William P.
Chamberlayne, John H.
Chamberlin, W. H.
Chambliss, T. E.
Chance, Mahlon
Chandler, Frank R.
Chandler, Parker C.
Chandler, William E.
Chandler, Zachariah
Chapin, E. N.
Chapin, John W.
Chapman, Albert J.
Chapman, Charles L.
Chapman, O. B.
Chapman, W. H.
Charities and Correction
Chase, Salmon P.
Chase, William Merritt
Chautauqua Association
Cheevers, Aurion V.
Cheney, T. S.

Cherokee Indians
Cherry, John H.
Chesebrough, A.
Chester, A.
Chester, J.
Chester, T. Morris
Chetlain, A. L.
Chickering, John W.
Chidlaw, B. W.
Childs, George W.
China
Chinese Immigration Question
Chisholm, I. W.
Chittenden, S. B.
Choate, D.
Choate, Joseph H.
Christie, D.
Christy, Robert
Chubb, Henry S.
Cincinnati Desiccating Company
Cincinnati Normal School
Cincinnati Post Office
Cincinnati, Society of
Cincinnati Society of Ex-Army and
    Navy Officers
Cincinnati Workingmen's Colonization
    Society
Cist, L. J.
Civil Service Reform
Civil Service Reform Association
Claflin, F. A.
Claflin, Mary B.
Claflin, William
Claflin University
Clague and Prindle
Clairborne, J. F. H.
Clapp, A. M.
Clark, Alexander
Clark, Andrew
Clark, Charles H.
Clark, Edward P.
Clark, Emmons
Clark, H. A.
Clark, P. M.
Clark University
Clarke, Daniel A.
Clarke, James Freeman
Clarke, Robert & Company
Clarke, Sylvester H.
Clarke, Thomas Allen
Clarke, William
Clarke, William W.
Clarkson, J. S.
Clarkson, Thomas
Clary, Dennison G.
Clay, Cassius M.
Clemens, S. L.
Clendenin, William
Cleveland Centennial

Cleveland City of
Cleveland Educational Bureau
Cleveland First Troop
Cleveland Light Guards
Clough, Isaac Story
Coates, B. F.
Cobb, H.
Cobden, Richard
Coburn, John
Cochran, R. H.
Cochrane, John
Cockrell, F. M.
Coe, George S.
Coffin, C. D.
Coffin, Charles F.
Coffin, E. G.
Coffin, Eugene
Coffin, H. W.
Coffrey, B. I.
Cohn, Henry S.
Coke, Richard
Cole, A. B.
Cole, A. N.
Cole, C.
Cole, W. T.
Colfax, Schuyler
Collett, Oscar W.
Collier, G. W.
Collier, Thomas S.
Collings, Henry
Collins, B.
Collins, C. T.
Collins, Charles L.
Collins, J. S.
Collins, Joseph B.
Collins, W. A.
Collins, William O.
Collis, Charles H. T.
Colonial Store Department—
    New South Wales
Colorado, Territory of
Colored Americans at the Banquet of
    Nations
Colquitt, Alfred H.
Colt, E. Boudinot
Columbian College of Citizenship
Columbus Board of Trade
Colver, E. M.
Comegys, C. G.
Comegys, W. H.
Comly, Guy S.
Comly, James M.
Comly, Susie A.
Commons, John R.
Compton, William M.
Comstock, Anthony
Conger, A. L.
Conger, H. N.
Conkling, Roscoe

Conley, John L.
Connecticut State of
Connecticut State Library
Connelly, William E.
Converse, Bolivar G.
Conway, Thomas W.
Conwell, Russell H.
Cook, Burton C.
Cook, C. C.
Cook, E. G.
Cook, Joel
Cook, Lemuel
Cook, Morris H.
Cooke, Jay
Cooley, Thomas M.
Cooper, B. F.
Cooper, Peter
Cooper, Sarah B.
Cooper Union
Cooperstown, (N. Y.)
Cope, Alexis
Corbin, D. G.
Corbin, David T.
Corbin, Fannie S.
Corbin, Henry C.
Corcoran, W. W.
Corcoran Gallery of Art
Corey, J. B.
Corkhill, George B.
Corkran, William
Cornell, A. B.
Cornell, Ezra
Cornell University
Cornell University Library
Corson, George N.
Corther, D. H.
Corwin, Ichabod
Corwine, Quinton
Corwine, R. M.
Cory, T. C.
Cotter, Oliver
Cottman, Thomas
Courtenay, William A.
Covell, H. J.
Covert, John C.
Covington, S. F.
Cowdrick, J. E.
Cowen, B. R.
Cowie, James
Cowlam, George B.
Cowles, Albert E.
Cowles, Edwin
Cowles, Henry
Cox, C. C.
Cox, Jacob D.
Cox, Joseph
Cox, S. S.
Coxe, John R.
Cracraft, J. W.

Cragin, Aaron H.
Cragin, E. F.
Crago, F. H.
Craig, Corydon F.
Craighead, S.
Crall, O. F.
Cramer, John T.
Crandall, H. B.
Crandall, Lee
Crane, C. H.
Crannell, W. W.
Crapo, William W.
Crapsey, Edward
Crawford, Norman S.
Creswell, D.
Creswell, John A. J.
Crilly, George
Crocker, Frank
Crocker, James C.
Croghan, George
Crook, Alja R.
Crook, George
Crook, Isaac
Crook, Mary Dailey
Crook, William H.
Crosby, H. S.
Crosby, Henry B.
Crosby, Joseph
Crosden, Hugh
Cross, E. L.
Crowder, Mattie Tomlin
Crowder, Thomas J.
Crump, William T.
Crutcher, Howard
Culley, Frank C.
Cullom, E. North
Cullom, S. M.
Culp, Edward C.
Culver, Austin B.
Culver, L. G.
Cumbach, Will
Cumberland, Army of
Cummings, J. W.
Cuneo
Cunningham, C. J. L.
Curry, J. L. M.
Curtis, George William
Curtis, Henry B.
Curtis, N. M.
Curtis, W. W.
Curtiss, H. W.
Cushing, Marshall
Cushman, A. S.
Custer National Monument Association
Cutler, Carroll
Cutler, James H.
Cutter, Norman
Cutts, J. Madison
Cuyler, Theodore L.

Dahlgren, Madeleine Vinton
Dakota, Territory of
Dallinger, Fred W.
Dalrymple, Ernest
Dalzell, James M.
Dana, Richard H. (Jr.)
Danford, L.
Dangler, D. A.
Daniels, Edward
Daniels, Rodney W.
Daniels, T. E.
Danner, John
Darr, Francis
Dassi, Giuse
Davidson, W. L.
Davis, C. K.
Davis, Charles C.
Davis, Charles W.
Davis, David
Davis, Edmund J.
Davis, Edward J.
Davis, George B.
Davis, H. G.
Davis, Horace
Davis, J. K.
Davis, J. N.
Davis, John
Davis, L. Clark
Davis, Murray
Davis, William E.
Davis, William Henry
Davis Island Dam
Dawes, E. C.
Dawes, H. L.
Dawson, George F.
Dawson, Henry B.
Day, Willard G.
Day, William
Dean, George W.
DeBebian, Louis
DeBois, W. E. B.
DeEmbil, M.
Defrees, John D.
DeGasparin, Agenor
Delano, C.
Deletombe, Alice S.
Dell, George A.
Deming, A. B.
Dennis, R. B.
Dennison, William
Deshler, W. G.
Detmers, H. J.
Devens, Charles
Devereux, J. H.
Devine, Thomas J.
Devol, H. F.
Devol, R. S.
Dewey, Melvil
DeWitt, F. H.

DeWolf, D. F.
DeWolfe, E. G.
Dexter, Julius
Deyo,Peter K.
Dichman, Ernest
Dickson, Palmer
Dickson, Samuel
Dickson, W. M.
Dillon J. Rhinelander
Dillon, John
Disney, William
District of Columbia
Dittenhoefer, A. J.
Dix, John A.
Dockery, O. H.
Dodds, Susannah W.
Dodge, J. R.
Dodge, William E.
Doggett, George F.
Donaldson, Thomas
Donan, P.
Dorsey, G. Volney
Dorsey, S. W.
Dougall, Allen H.
Douglas William G.
Douglass, Frederick
Dowling, P. H.
Downing, George T.
Doyle, John
Drake, E. F.
Drake, Frank M.
Drake, John B.
Drake, Samuel
Drexel, A. J.
Drum, R. C.
DuBois, James T.
Dudley, M. S.
Dudley, Thomas W.
Dudley, William W.
Duffy, Charles
Duluth Petition
Duluth State Bank
Dun R. G. and Company
Dunbar, W.
Duncan, Blanton
Dundore, F.
Dunn, W. M.
Dutcher, Silas B.
Duval, I. H.
Dwight, J. W.
Dyke, H. Hart
Dymond, Richard

Eads, James B.
Earl, W. C.
Earle, William E.
Earnshaw, Margaret A.
Earnshaw, William
Eastman, Z.

Eaton, D. B.
Eaton, John
  Boston, Mass.
Eaton, John
  Washington, D. C.
Eaton, T. T.
Edgerton, Lycurgus
Edgerton, R. A.
Edmunds, George F.
Edmunds, Henry R.
Edmunds, J. M.
Eells, Dan P.
Eggers, Ernst A.
Eldred, J. E.
Eliot, Charles W.
Elkinton, Joseph S.
Ellen, J. S.
Elliot, George H.
Elliott, E. B.
Elliott, P. A.
Elliott, Robert B.
Ellis, Charles
Ellis, John W.
Ellsworth, W. L.
Ely, George H.
Ely, Heman
Ely, Seneca W.
Emancipation Proclamation
Emory College
Enochs, W. H.
Errett, Russell
Eshman, Michael W.
Estill, J. H.
Estill, W. H.
Evans, F. S.
Evans, N. W.
Evarts, Helen Minerva
Evarts,Mary
Evarts, William M.
Everett, Edward
Everett, Edward H.
Everhart, J. B.
Everitt, L. H.
Evers, C. W.
Ewart, Thomas W.
Ewell, J. L.
Ewing, E. E.
Ewing, Thomas
Ewing, William

Faenicke, Gustave
Fairbanks, C. W.
Fairbanks, Horace
Fairchild, Lucius
Farnham, J. E. C.
Farquhar, A. B.
Farrow, Henry P.
Farwell, C. B.
Farwell, John V.

Fassett, C. Adele
Fay, G. O.
Fellows, E. F.
Felton, Charles E.
Felton, William H.
Fenton, R. O.
Ferguson, E. A.
Fernow, B.
Ferris, Morris P. (Mrs.)
Ferry, T. W.
Fessenden, W. P.
Field, Cyrus W.
Fifth Army Corps—Society of
Filley, Chauncey
Fillmore, E. E.
Filson, C. P.
Finch, George M.
Finnell, John W.
Firestone, C. D.
Fish, Hamilton
Fishback, William
Fisher, B. F.
Fisher, C. W.
Fisher, Phil D.
Fisher, S. S.
Fisk, A. C.
Fisk, Clinton B.
Fiske, L. R.
Fiske, Willard
Fitch, M. W.
Fithian, Freeman J.
Fitts, Harvey E.
Fitzgerald, Thomas
Fitzsimons, V. P.
Flagler, Benjamin
Florida Election Frauds
Florida, State of
Folger, R. H.
Folger, W. B.
Follett, O.
Fonda, Charles W.
Foos, Rodney
Foote, Emma
Foote, John A.
Foraker, J. B.
Forbes, J. M.
Forbes, W. W.
Force, M. F.
Ford, C. W.
Ford, George H.
Forney, John W.
Forrester, Charles
Forster, George H.
Forster, William
Foster, Charles
Foster, E. H.
Foster, Frank T.
Foster, John W.

Foster, Morrison
Foster, William L.
Fox, Cyrus T.
Fralick, I. W.
Francisco, A. W.
Frazer, Abner L.
Frazier, John W.
Freedmen's Aid and Southern
    Education Society
Freeman, Pliny
Frelinghuysen, Frederick T.
Fremont, J. C.
Fremont, Jessie Benton (Mrs. J. C.)
Fremont, City of
French, Charles W.
French, George A.
French, H. F.
French, R. S.
French, William H.
Freyre, C. Santander de
Frost, Henry A.
Frothingham, Richard
Fry, W. F.
Fry, W. N.
Frye, William P.
Fuller, John W.
Fulton, Charles C.
Fulweiler, C. H.
Furay, William S.

Gaines, William
Gallagher, T. J.
Galt, William R.
Gangwer, A. M.
Gano, J.
Gano, John A.
Gara, Isaac B.
Gardiner, Asa Bird
Gardiner, E. T.
Gardiner, John
Gardner, H. S.
Gardner, Robert Skiles
Garfield, James A.
Garfield, Lucretia R.
Garfield Monument Fund
Garland, A. H.
Garret, Philip C.
Garretson, A. S.
Garrison, C. W.
Garvey, William M.
Gayarre, Charles
Gaylor, J.
Geary, John W.
Geiger, Joseph H.
George, Austin
Georgia, State of
Georgia State Agricultural Society
Getty, George D.
Getz, Owen B.

Gibbons, Charles
Gibbs, F. C.
Gibson, R. L.
Gibson, W. H.
Giebel, F. J.
Gifford, W. C.
Gilbert, William J.
Gilden, Dan R.
Gilder, R. W.
Gilkey, E. Howard
Gilman, D. C.
Gilmore, Charles D.
Gilpin, Charles
Gilstrap, A. L.
Gitchell, J. M.
Gladden, Washington
Gladwin, Edgar F.
Glasgow, S. L.
Glassie, D. W.
Glenn, James K.
Glidden, K. B.
Glover, J. M.
Goddard, C. W.
Goddard, Charles
Goddard, S. A.
Godfrey, Thomas J.
Godkin, E. L.
Godman, W. D.
Goepper, M.
Goff, N.
Gompers, Samuel
Goode, Samuel
Goodloe, William Cassius
Goodman, A. T.
Goodrich, R. C.
Goodwin, T. S.
Goodwin, William P.
Gordon, J. B.
Gordon, Thomas W.
Goshorn, A. F.
Gossman, George
Gould, F. A.
Gould, Jay
Gould, John M.
Gould, R. de Tracy
Goulding, J. H.
Graef, Arnold
Grafton, William T.
Graham, A. A.
Graham, William F.
Grand Army of the Republic
          Memorial Services
          National Encampments
          National Headquarters
          State Organizations by States
Granger, Moses M.
Grant, Frederick Dent
Grant, Ulysses S.
Grant Monument Association

Gray, Alex T.
Gray, D. S.
Gray, H. G.
Gray, J. R.
Gray, N. A.
Grayson, Salathiel
Green, F. W.
Green, Jesse C.
Green, John H.
Green, Samuel A.
Green Springs Academy
Greene, J. B.
Greene, Roger S.
Greiner, H. C.
Grier, John A.
Griffin, Albert
Griffith, G. S.
Griffith, W. W.
Griffith, William E.
Griswold, L. D.
Griswold, S. O.
Grosvenor, Charles
Grow, Galusha A.
Grubb, Joseph C.
Gruell, N. R.
Guiteau, John
Gunckel, Lewis B.
Gundry, Richard
Gustin, George A.

Hafford, Ferris F.
Hagans, M. B.
Hahn, Ralph H.
Halderman, W. N.
Hale, Edward E.
Hale, Eugene
Hale, M. C.
Hale, Matthew
Hale, Sarah J.
Hale, William B.
Haley, A. G.
Halford, E. M.
Hall, Caleb G.
Hall, George Edward
Hall, H. Clay
Hall, J. G.
Hall, John
Halleck, Fitz-Greene
Halstead, M.
Ham, Charles H.
Hamilton, J. K.
Hamilton. John C.
Hamlin, H.
Hammill, Cordie Glenn
Hammill, George C.
Hammitt, S. Scott
Hammond, Eli Whitney
Hampton, Wade
Hampton Normal and
          Agricultural Institute

Hanchett, John T.
Hancock, John—Ohio
Hancock, John—Texas
Hancock, Winfield Scott
Handy, Thomas H.
Hanna, Mark A.
Hannan, J. W.
Harbaugh, Mary C.
Harbaugh, S. G.
Harlan, George W.
Harlan, James
Harlan, John M.
Harlan, Robert
Harmer, A. C.
Harmon, John C.
Harper, J. J.
Harper, Rice
Harriman, Walter
Harrington, G. D.
Harrington, J. G.
Harris, L. T.
Harris, Nathaniel R.
Harris, T. M.
Harris, William Hamilton
Harris, William R.
Harrison, Benjamin
Harrison, Lynde
Hart, Alphonso
Hart, Roswell
Hartman, Samuel
Hartranft, J. F.
Hartshorn, O. N.
Harvard University
Harvey, F. L.
Haskell, Charles C.
Haskell, Dudley C.
Haskell, T. N.
Hastie, William S.
Hastings, Russell
Hatch, Francis H.
Hatch, H. F.
Hatfield, R. M.
Hathaway, John R.
Hatton, Frank
Hause, Henry K.
Haviland C. Augustus
Haviland, Francis
Hawes, Solomon R.
Hawkins, Alvin
Hawkins, Dexter A.
Hawkins, Gardner C.
Hawkins, J. H.
Hawley, John B.
Hawley, Joseph R.
Hay, Charles
Hay, John
Hayden, F. V.
Hayden, H. C.

Hayden, Horace Edward
Hayeden, Joseph E.
Hayeen, S. L.
Hayes, C. W.
Hayes, R. T.
Hayes, Rutherford B.
 Correspondence — Original letters or drafts; arranged alphabetically by name of correspondent.
 Correspondence—Copies used by Mr. Williams in preparing the life of Mr. Hayes; arranged chronologically.
 Messages and speeches—arranged by subject or occasion; notes, drafts and printed copies.
 Miscellaneous — Cabinet Notes, law cases, and material that might have interest to a biographer.
Haygood, A. G.
Haynes, William E.
Hays, James
Hays, Samuel
Hazen, W. B.
Head, Natt
Heald, J. T.
Healey, James H.
Healy, W. H.
Heath, Thomas T.
Heath, William M.
Hedges, Henry C.
Hedges, Robert
Hedges, William C.
Helfenstein, William L.
Helper, Hinton Rowan
Henderson, D. C.
Henderson, John
Henderson, John B.
Henderson, W. F.
Hendley, C. M.
Hendricks, Thomas A.
Henry, E. P.
Henry, Edward E.
Henry, William D.
Hereford, Frank
Herrick, J. F.
Herrick, Myron T.
Herron, Harriet C.
Herron, John W.
Herron, W. A.
Hertwig, John George
Herzing, P. W.
Hester, William
Heyl, Lewis
Hibbard, B. L.
Hickenlooper, A.
Hickok, Frank
Hicks, G. W.
Hiett, J. W.
Higgins, M. L.

Ide, G. E.
Ide, Harriet E.
Illinois, State of
Imboden, J. D.
Importers and Grocers Board of Trade
Independent Order of Good Templars (The)
Independent Order of Odd Fellows
Independent Republican (The)
Indian Affairs—Proclamations
Indian Treaties—Ohio
Indian—Miscellaneous
Indiana, State of
Ingalls, John J.
Ingersoll, Robert G.
Inter-Oceanic Canal—Miscellaneous
International Exhibition 1876
International League
Iowa, State of
Irelan, J. R.
Irish, O. H.
Isaacs, Myer S.
Isenberg, J. G.
Ittner, Anthony

Jackson, Andrew
Jackson, J. P.
Jackson, John J.
Jacob, Charles
Jacob, Charles D.
Jacobi, M. A.
Jacobson, Augustus
James, Benjamin F.
James, Charles P.
James, Darwin R.
James, Edmund J.
James, John H.
James, Thomas L.
Jameson, John A.
Jarvis, Kent
Jay, John
Jaynes, A. D.
Jefferson, Thomas
Jefferson County—Ohio
Jenkins, G. W.
Jennings, W. H.
Jesup, Morris K
Jewell, Marshall
Jewett, W. Cornell
Joel, Joseph A.
Johanna, King of
Johnes, George W.
Johns, H. T.
Johnson, Andrew
Johnson, Eli
Johnson, Fred·
Johnson, Henry
Johnson, Henry K.
Johnson, Jasper W.

Johnson, Oliver
Johnson, R. U.
Johnson, Reverdy
Johnson, T. F.
Johnson, W. W.
Johnston, Alexander
Johnston, David
Johnston, Edwin L.
Johnston, John W.
Johnston, William
Johnston, William A.
Johnstone, Robert
Jones, Albert G.
Jones, Frank W.
Jones, George W.
Jones, J. R.
Jones, J. W.
Jones, John D.
Jones, John Paul
Jones, Lucien C.
Jones, T. C.
Jones, T. D.
Jones, Thomas M.
Jones, W. P.
Jones, W. W.
Jordan, Francis

Kane, Thomas L.
Kansas, State of
Kansas, State Historical Society
Kansas, State Temperance Union
Karr, Charles W.·
Karr, John
Kasson, John A.
Kaufman, P. J.
Kearney, E. S.
Keck, J. L.
Kedzie, J. H.
Keffer, J. C.
Keifer, J. Warren
Keirle, William F.
Kellar, A. J.
Keller, A. R.
Kelley, B. F.
Kelley, William D.
Kellicott, D. S.
Kellogg, A. G.
Kellogg, William P.
Kelly, John
Kelly, William D.
Kelser, J. J.
Kemper, Andrew C.
Kenaday, A. M.
Kendall, F. A.
Kennan, C. L.
Kennedy, Joseph C. G.
Kennedy, Robert P.
Kennett, H. G.
Kennon, L. W. V.

enyon College
eogh, Thomas B.
ey, David M.
eyes, E. W.
eyser, William
ibler, Charles H.
  breth, John C.
illam, Benjamin
illgore, Joseph L.
illip, W. W.
ilpatrick, Judson
  " ball, E.
   ball, F. M.
   ball, H. I.
  mball, H. P.
 imball, S. I.
imberland, Daniel
imberley, D. H.
ing, Charles
ing, Clarence A.
ing, D. L.
ing, Hezekiah
ing, Horatio C.
ing, John E.
ing, Rufus
 "ng, William F.
inney, Coates
'insman, F.
'irby, D. P.
'irk, R. C.
'irk, S. D.
'irk, William
'irksey, I. J.
'irkwood, Samuel J.
'ittredge, E. W.
'napp, H. S.
'napp, Henry F.
'napp, W. A.
'night, George W.
'nox, John Jay

,abor League—United States of America
,afayette College
,aFayette Monument
,aflin, A. H.
,akeside Assembly
,amar, L. Q. C.
,amb, Martha J.
,amon, Ward H.
,anahan, John
,and Grants
,andon, Melville S.
,ane, Ebenezer
,ane, William G.
,ang, Carl F.
,angston, John M.
,anman, Charles
,apham, E. G.
,arned, E. C.

Latham, George R.
Latimer, C. S.
Latrobe, Ferdinand C.
Latty, A. S.
Lauer, Paul E.
Lawrence, C. B.
Lawrence, William
Lawton, Winborn
Lea, Henry C.
Leake, Joseph B.
Leavenworth, E. W.
LeDoyen, F.
LeDuc, William G.
Lee, Alfred E.
Lee, J. M.
Lee, John C.
Leech, Samuel V.
Leffingwell, A. Tracy
Leggett, M. D.
Lehmaier, James S.
Leland, Frank
Lemmon, John M.
Lemon, George E.
Leonard, W. E.
Leppelman, L.
Leroy, James
Lesher, D.
Leslie, C. P.
Lester, C. Edwards
Leue, Adolph
Lewis, B. W.
Lewis, David P.
Lewis, T. M.
Lewis, William G. W.
Lewton, Lewis
L'Hommedier, S. S.
Lieber, Francis
Lilly, E. A.
Lincoln, Abraham
Lincoln, M. D. (Mrs.)
Lincoln, Robert T.
Linderman, Henry
Linton, Irvin B.
Little, John A.
Littlefield, R. S.
Livingston, John
Lloyd, Richard
Locke, R. D.
Lockwood, Belva A.
Lockwood, E. Dunbar
Logan, John A.
London, William
Long, James F.
Long, John D.
Long, John F.
Long, Sydney C.
Longworth, Nicholas
Looker, Thomas H.
Lord, Henry W.

McPherson, Edward
McPherson, James B.
McQuigg, William T.
McRae, A. S.
McWhorter, H. C.
Mead, Edward
Mead, Fred G.
Mead, Larkin
Meade, Nathaniel B.
Mears, W. E.
Medill, Joseph
Meek, B.
Meharry Medical College
Meigs, M. C.
Melton, Samuel W.
Melvin, Thayer
Merchant, W. B.
Meredith, John A.
Merrill, C. E.
Merrill, P.
Merritt, E. A.
Metcalf, E. W.
Methodist Episcopal Church
Meyer, John M.
Michaelis, R.
Michigan—17th Regiment
Michigan, State of
Middleton, D. W.
Miles, Nelson A.
Military Order of the Loyal Legion
    Commandery-in-Chief
    State Commanderies (by State)
Millen, H. A.
Miller, A. H.
Miller, A. P.
Miller, E. P.
Miller, George A. Q.
Miller, J. DeWitt
Miller, Joaquin
Miller, Sam F.
Milliken, James
Mills, Clark
Mills, L. A.
Mills, Lewis E.
Miner, I. L.
Minnesota, State of
Missouri, Historical Society
Missouri, State of
Mitchell, George
Mitchell, John
Mitchell, John H.
Mitchell, N. M.
Mitchell, W. E.
Mittleberger, Augusta
Mizener, D. A.
Mohonk Conference
Mohun, Claire Hanson
Monroe, Henrietta L.
Monroe, James

Montague, D.
Montana, Territory of
Montgomery, C. M.
Montross, John T.
Moore, David H.
Moore, Hugh
Moore, J. P.
Moore, R. B.
Moore, Thomas
Moore, William H.
Morgan, C. H.
Morgan, E. D.
Morgan, George W.
Morgan, John T.
Morgan, Thomas P.
Mormonism
Morrill, Job M.
Morrill, Justin S.
Morris, Fenton M.
Morris, I. N.
Morris, P. Pemberton
Morris, Samuel
Morris, W. J.
Morris, William Gouverneur
Morrison, George
Morrison, Leonard
Morse, Isaac S.
Morse, Leopold
Morton, Henry C.
Morton, John M.
Morton, Levi P.
Morton, Oliver P.
Morton, Oliver T.
Mosby, John S.
Moss, Fannie
Moss, Jay O.
Moulton, C. W.
Mount Union College
Murphy, Francis
Murphy, Jere
Murphy, R. C.
Murray, Eli H.
Muskogee Nation
Mussey, R. D.
Myer, Albert J.
Myers, Henry C.

Napier, H. H.
Nash, E. W.
Nash, George K.
Nash, Simeon
Nashville, City of
National Academy of Sciences
National Agricultural Society
National Civil Service Reform League
National Educational Association
National Fair Association
National Home for Disabled Volunteer
    Soldiers

National Immigration Bureau
National Law University
National Normal University
National Prison Association
National Reform Association
National Temperance Convention
Naughten, James
Navy Department
Neal, H. S.
Neall, Isaac J.
Neely, F. T.
Neer, J. O.
Neff, William H.
Negley, James S.
Neil, John B.
Nelson, E. T.
Nelson, Henry A.
Neosho Valley District Fair Association
Nessle, J. B.
Nessle, W. H.
Nettleton, A. B.
Neubert, H. G.
Nevada, State of
New England Chautauqua
New England Historic Genealogical Society
New England Monument Company
New England Society of the City of New York
New Hampshire, State of
New Hampshire, Veterans Association
New Jersey, State of
New York Chamber of Commerce
New York Christian Home for Intemperate Men
New York Custom House
New York National Guard
New York Press Association
New York, State of
Newark, City of
Newberry, J. S.
Newberry, John S.
Newcomb, Simon
Newcomer, James K.
Newell, William A.
Newkirk, Garrett
Newspaper Clippings—Miscellaneous
Newton, Frances E.
Newton, Isaac
Nicholls, Francis T.
Nichols, C. M.
Nicholson, Joseph
Nicholson, W. L.
Nickerson, A. H.
Nigh, Elias
Nimmo, J.
Noah, J. J.
Noble, Henry
Noble, William
Nolan, Dennis E.

Norcross, J.
Nordhoff, Charles
North, A. C.
Northcott, R. S.
Northrop, L. C.
Northwestern Ohio Natural Gas Company
Norton, A. B.
Norton, C. B.
Noyes, Charles R.
Noyes, E. H.
Noyes, Edward F.
Noyes, John H.
Nye, A. T.
Nye, R. L.

Oberlin College
O'Connor, Paul
Oglesby, J. H.
Oglesby, Richard J.
Ohio Board of State Charities
Ohio Centennial
Ohio—Fifth Amendment
Ohio General Assembly
Ohio Geological Surveys
Ohio Institution for the Blind
Ohio Institutions and Charities
Ohio Legislative Expenses
Ohio National Guard
Ohio Republican Committee
Ohio Republican League
Ohio Society of Chicago
Ohio Society of New York
Ohio Soldiers Orphans Home
Ohio, State of
Ohio State Archaeological and Historical Society
Ohio State Penitentiary
Ohio State University
Ohio Wesleyan University
O'Kane, Bernard
Oldest Inhabitant Association District of Columbia
Oliver, James
Oliver, John F.
Omaha Scandal
O'Neall, Joseph W.
O'Neill, Charles
Onlahan, Richard
Ordway, N. G.
Oregon, State of
Orton, Edward
Osborn, Thomas A.
Ostrander, Eliza
Otis, Harrison G.
Otis, L. B.
Ott, John
Otto, W. T.
Overdier, David

H. C.
Mary L.
Sherman S.
W. B.
W. K.
W. K. (Jr.)
William B.
James S.
e, Henry
Jacob
. Henry
William Oscar
lt, Theodore
ariah S.
mes P.

ns, W. S.
ldt, Charles
John E.
mes W.
atilda H.
. W.
ld, J. B.
Ellen Miner
William M. F.
drew
ociety for the Prevention of Cruelty
nimals
). W.
Thomas H.
;, S. Kellogg
rod, J. K.
Benjamin P.
ohn
Alfred
Otis H.
. L. (Mrs. R. S.)
ord, George V.
ord, George W.

Chauncey B.
oseph
H.
E. B.
eorge R.
, Gustavus
, John P.
s Agricultural & Mechanical
ciation
s National Guard
. C.
rino, Republic of
, F. B.
. C.
cy County—Ohio
, H. S.
arbara, City of
, A. A.
, C. H.

Sargent, George B.
Sargent, Horace Binney
Sarony
Saunders, Alvin
Saunders, Thomas J.
Savage, Helen I.
Saville, J. H.
Saxton, Rufus
Scammon, E. P.
Scammon, J. Young
Scanlon, Michael
Schell, A.
Schenck, Robert C.
Schermes, G.
Schley, William Louis
Schneider, Edward F.
Schofield, J. M.
Schroeder, Henry
Schroeder, John E.
Schumacher, John
Schurz, Carl
Scofield, Levi T.
Scott, C. F.
Scott, Henry W.
Scott, J.
Scott, Robert N.
Scott, Rufus
Scott, Thomas A.
Scott, W. H.
Scovel, J. M.
Scovel, Sylvester
Scudder, Horace E.
Seaman, Frank
Seelye, Julius H.
Seibert, S. H.
Seip, Albert N.
Selkirk, Charles F.
Sessions, F. C.
Severson, Benjamin
Sewall, T. O.
Seward, F. W.
Seward, George F.
Shannon, T. B.
Sharp, Charles
Sharpe, Alfred C.
Shaw, Albert D.
Shaw, W. L.
Sheffield, William
Sheldon, George
Sheldon, H. G.
Sheldon, L. A.
Shell, Jonathan
Shellabarger, Samuel
Shenandoah, Army of the
Shepard, A. D.
Shepard, Elliott F.
Shepardson, Norris H.
Sheppard, Thomas J.
Sheridan, Andrew

Sheridan, George A.
Sheridan, Philip H.
Sherman, John
Sherman, N. G.
Sherman, W. J.
Sherman, William T.
Sherwood, Kate B.
Shields, George H.
Shipherd, Jacob R.
Shipley, Murray
Shirley, George B.
Shoemaker, Samuel M.
Sickel, H. G.
Sickels, David B.
Siddons, J. H.
Siebert, Wilbur H.
Simmons, J. F.
Simmons, William A.
Simon, Edward
Simpson, M. V.
Simpson, Mathew
Simpson, W. H.
Sinclair, Samuel
Skiles, J. W.
Skinner, B. M.
Skinner, Joseph J.
Slade, James P.
Slafter, Edmund F.
Slane, Jackson
Slayton, H. K.
Slemmons, John P.
Slider, T. P.
Sloan, W. B.
Sloanaker, A. B.
Slocum, H. W.
Slough, Martin
Small, R. B. (Jr.)
Smedley, A.
Smiley, A. K.
Smith, Allen (Jr.)
Smith, Allie
Smith, Charles E.
Smith, Charles H.
Smith, Charlotte
Smith, Courtland H.
Smith, D. R.
Smith, Delevan
Smith, Edward
Smith, Egbert T.
Smith, Electa E.
Smith, Frank W.
Smith, Fred H.
Smith, George P.
Smith, Green Clay
Smith, Harry Eaton
Smith, Harry R.
Smith, Howard B.
Smith, I. Q.
Smith, James A.

Smith, James H.
Smith, Joseph P.
Smith, L.
Smith, Prosper A.
Smith, Richard
Smith, Roswell
Smith, T. C. H.
Smith, William E.
Smith, William Henry
    Correspondence
    Conversations
    Newspaper Clippings
    Notes
Smithsonian Institution
Smithton, F. G.
Smoot, S. S.
Smyrna—Archbishop of
Snead, Austine
Snohomish Indians
Snowden, A. Loudon
Sons of Revolutionary Sires
Sons of Temperance
Sons of the American Revolution—
    Society of
Sons of Veterans
Soule, N. E.
South Carolina, State of
South Dakota, State of
Southard, Sidney M.
Southern Republican Association
Southwestern Soldiers Association
Spalding, B. P.
Spalding, W. F.
Spangler, E. T.
Spates, A. Worth
Speakman, Thomas H.
Speer, W.
Spencer, George E.
Spencer, Richard
Sperry, C. A.
Spiegel Grove
Spinner, F. E.
Spinner, R. E.
Spofford, A. R.
Spooner, Thomas
Sprague, A. P.
Stafford, Samuel B.
Stagg, Abraham
Stanbery, Henry
Standefer, Lemuel J.
Stanton, Edwin L.
Stanton, Edwin M.
Stanton, William
Stanwood, James B.
Starr, A. A.
Statistics, Bureau of
Stearns, Charles
Stearns, M. L.
Steel, Edward T.

Turner, T. M.
Turney, Joseph
Turney, Samuel D.
Tutton, A. P.
Twining, Alexander C.
Tyler, E. B.
Tyler, Erastus D.
Tyler, John—New York
Tyler, John—Virginia
Tyner, James N.

Ullman, Daniel
Updegraff, J. T.
Upson, William H.
Urner, Milton G.
Union League Clubs
Union Prisoners of War National Memorial
Union Soldiers Association
Union Veterans Club
Union Veterans Union
United Labor League of America
United States Board of Trade
Utah, Territory of

Vallette, Maria
Vance, A.
Vance, William J.
Van Deman, J. D.
Van Deman, J. H.
Van Horn, Burt
Van Voorhis, John
Van Wyck, C. H.
Van Zandt, Charles C.
Veeder, John W.
Vernon, James M.
Verree, John P.
Veterans of the Mexican, Black Hawk and
   Florida Wars
Vincent, George E.
Virginia, Commonwealth of
Vorhes, Austin W.

Wade, B. F.
Wade, Winthrop
Wadsworth, William R.
Wagenhals, P. M.
Waggoner, Clarke
Waggoner, Ralph
Wagner, Louis
Wahle, G. R.
Wainwright, George W.
Wait, John T.
Waite, Alfred T.
Waite, M. R.
Walbridge, H. S.
Walcutt, Charles C.
Wales, S. H.
Walker, Alexander
Walker, F. A.

Walker, George
Walker, M. B.
Walker, Mary E. (Dr.)
Wallace, Lew
Wallace, R. M.
Wanamaker, John
Ward, A. G. Dudley
Ward, William H.
Warden, William W.
Warder, J. A.
Warmoth, H. C.
Warner, C. L.
Warner, Willard
Washburn, C. C.
Washburn, J. D.
Washburne, Elihu B.
Washington, Booker T.
Washington, George
Washington Monument Commission
Washington, Territory of
Wasson, W. H.
Watrous, J. A.
Watson, Augustus
Watson, C. K.
Watterson, Henry
Wauseon (Ohio) Post Office
Wayland, E. L.
Wayland, Francis
Wayman, A. W.
Webb, Isaac
Webb Family Genealogy
Webber, C. T.
Weber, E. L.
Weed, Thurlow
Weeks, Joseph D.
Weeks, Ralph J.
Weideman, U. M.
Weir, L. C.
Welker, Martin
Welles, Gideon
Wells, David A.
Wells, J. Madison
Welsh, James H.
Welsh, John
West, J. R.
West Point
West Virginia—Society of Army of
Western Biographical Publishing Company
Western Reserve University
Wharton, Jack
Wharton, Joseph
Wheeler, William A.
Wheeless, John P.
Whipple, H. B.
White, Andrew D.
White, Julius
White, Robert
White, William J. P.
Whitley, William H.

. F.
C.
alt

.
n Greenleaf
harles
P.
. A.
illiam C.

C.

:s B.
hall P.
as F.

rge
oward
rles A.
cis E.
ilton
. H.
fred
G.
P.
iarles R.
H.
:lia
:orge B.
:orge H.
:orge W.
re N.
:wis C.
. G.
. W.
Alex
J. A.
M. T.
orge W.
in

W.
ord
rles G.
`all
es F.
es Grant
es M.
es W.
ι A.
.ey L.
iam S.
lliam

H.

Wingard, S. C.
Winship, John O.
Winslow, Edwin
Winsmith, J. C.
Winstead, George W.
Winthrop, Robert
Wisconsin, State of
Wishart, A.
Witcher, John S.
Withers, A. Q.
Wolcott, James L.
Wolcott, Samuel
Wolf, S.
Wolff, John B.
Womans Home Missionary Society
Womans Relief Corps
Womens Christian Temperance Union
Wood, E. E.
Wood, Frederick W.
Wood, Horatio
Wood, John B.
Wood, Thomas J.
Wood, William P.
Woodford, Stewart L.
Woodhouse, Charles
Woodruff, James O.
Woods, Albert B.
Woods, George L.
Woods, W. B.
Woodward, W. W.
Woodward, William
Woodworth, J. M.
Woodworth, L. D.
Work, J. B.
Worthington, T.
Wright, B. H.
Wright, Craft I.
Wright, D. Thew
Wright, George B.
Wright, Marcus J.
Wyoming, Territory of

Yale, Elihu
Yale Alumni Association
Yale College
Yates, Richard
Yeatman, James E.
Yeatman, R. T.
Yorktown National Centennial
    Surrender of Cornwallis
Yorston, John C.
Yoston, S. M.
Young, Charles L.
Young, John Russell
Young, Thomas L.
Yuram, Jason

CORRESPONDENCE BETWEEN MEMBERS OF THE HAYES FAMILY

Austin, Alven
Austin, C. D.
Austin, L. C.

Bancroft, William
Bigelow, Mary A.
Bigelow, Russell A.
Birchard Family
Birchard, A. T.
Birchard, Austin to
    Birchard, Mary
    Birchard, Sardis
    Hayes, Rutherford B.
    Hayes, Webb C.
Birchard, Charles A.
Birchard, Mary to
    Birchard, Austin
    Birchard, Sardis
    Hayes, Lucy Webb
    Hayes, Rutherford B.
Birchard, Mary A. to
    Hayes, Rutherford B.
Birchard, Sardis to
    Birchard, Austin
    Hayes, Rutherford B.
Boggs, Lemuel
Boggs, Margaret
Boggs, Scott C.
Breckinridge, Mary D.

Cook, Adda
Cook, Ellen T.
Cook Family—Genealogy
Cook, Lucy
Cook, M. S.
Cook, Margaret
Cook, Maria
Cook, Nell
Cook, Phoebe
Cook, S. M.

Davis, Eliza G.
Day, J. Warren D.
DeWitt, Charlott P.
DeWitt, John C.
DeWitt, R. B.
DeWitt, R. C.

Elliot, C. S.
Elliot, Henry R.

Fitch, Mary M.
Fullerton, E. B.

Fullerton, Fanny
Fullerton, J. S.

Gilmore, F. T.
Gilmore, Margaret C.
Glenn, Emma Foote
Grant, Sarah J.

Hastings, Emily
Hayes, Birchard A. to
    Hayes, Lucy Webb
    Hayes, Rutherford B.
Hayes, Fanny R. to
    Hayes, Lucy Webb
    Hayes, Rutherford B.
    Hayes, Rutherford P.
    Hayes, Scott Russell
    Hayes, Webb Cook
Hayes, Lucy Webb to
    Birchard, Sardis
    Children
Hayes, Mary Miller
Hayes, Mary Sherman
Hayes, Rutherford Platt
Hayes, Scott Russell
Hayes, Sophia Birchard to
    Birchard, Sardis
    Hayes, Lucy Webb
    Hayes, Rutherford B.
Hayes, Webb Cook
Herron, Harriet C.
Howells, Mildred
Huntington, Adda Cook

Jewett, Ellen R.
Jewett, John N.

Keeler, Isaac M.
Keeler, J. E.
Keeler, Lucy E.
Kilbourne, S. M.

McCandless, Lucy H. C.
McFarland, Lucy
McFarland, Mary E.
McKell, Ella C.
McKell, James
McKell, Joseph
McKell, Phoebe
McKell, Thomas G.
McLellan B.
Mead, Charles L.
Mead, Larkin G.

Mitchell, Jean
Mitchell, John G.
Mitchell, Laura P.
Mitchell, Lily
Mosher, M. D. (Mrs.)

Nelson, Isaac C.
Nelson John F.
Noyes, H. S.

Platt, Emily
Platt, Fanny Hayes
Platt, Rutherford H.
Platt, Sarah F. (Mrs. W. A.)
Platt, Susan
Platt, W. A.

Scott, J. W.
Scott, Joseph T.
Shepard, Elinor M.
Shepard, Joanna M.
Smith, Sophia E.
Stilwell, Kate F.
Ware, J. W.
Warren, Abby
Webb, J. T.
Webb, Joseph T. to
    Hayes Children
    Hayes, Lucy Webb
    Hayes, Rutherford B.
    Webb, Maria
Webb, James D.
Webb, Maria

LIST OF IMPORTANT NAMES IN CORRESPONDENCE
OF LUCY WEBB HAYES

American McAll Association
Andrews, E. F.
Andrews, Emma S.
Anthony, Susan B.
Armstrong, Sallie D.
Astor, Augusta
Austin, Emily L.
Austin, L.

Bacon, Connie M.
Bailey, M. B.
Ballinger, Betty
Ballinger, Hally
Bancroft, Elizabeth
Bascom, William F.
Baxter, J. H.
Bergland, Lucy
Birchard, S.
Bodley, Rachel L.
Boggs, Fannie
Boggs, Margaret Cook
Boggs, Sallie T.
Booth, E. G.
Breckenridge, Louise D.
Bryan, Guy M.
Bryan, Rose L.
Bryant, William Cullen
Bruce, B. K. (Mrs.)
Burnside, A. E.
Burrell, Eliza
Bynum, James

Carlisle, Lucy M.
Carter, Isabel
Casey, Emma W.

Casey, Thomas Lincoln
Chalker, A. N. (Mrs.)
Chapin, Sallie F.
Chittenden, Cornelia B.
Claflin, Mary B.
Claney, William M.
Clark, A. Louisa (Mrs. A. R.)
Clark, Rush (Mrs.)
Clemmer, Mary
Collins, Helen K.
Comly, Elizabeth M. (Mrs. J. M.)
Cone, Mary E. Thropp
Conger, Stella B.
Connelly, M.A. (Mrs.)
Cook, Adda
Cook, Diathea
Cook, Lucy H.
Cook, Margaret L.
Cook, Maria W.
Cook, Nellie S.
Cooper, Sarah B.
Corbin, Frances E.
Corning, J. Leonard
Cory, E. G.
Cracroft, Louise D.
Crook, Mary D.
Cutler, Louise
Cuyler, Theodore L.
Dahlgren, Madeleine Vinton
Dall, Caroline H.
Dalles Blue Ribbon Club
Davis, Edith K.
Davis, Eliza G. (Mrs. John)
Davis, Elizabeth (Mrs.)
Dawes, E. S.

Dawes, E. S. (Mrs.)
Deale, William G.
Devens Family
Dewey, Annie
DeWitt, Charlotte
Dix, Catherine M.
Dix, John A.
Dodge, W. C.
Dorsey, Anna H.

Eaton, John
Edes, Margaret
Elliot, Henry R.
Ellis, Anne
Ellis, Caroline S. L.
Evarts Family

Fagan, Charles
Fairbanks, Horace (Mrs.)
Felton, W. H.
Ferriss, C. W.
Ferriss, Cornelia W.
Fisk, Clinton B.
Foote, Emma
Force, Frances H.
Force, M. F.
Ford, Harriet E.
Fremont, Jessie Benton
Fry, Henry L.
Fullerton, Fannie
Fullerton, J. F.

Gilmore, Margaret Cook
Glenn, Emma Foote
Good Templars—California
Gouverneur, M.
Greenleaf, J. W.
Guthrie, S. S.

Hall, George C.
Hallowell, Sarah C. F.
Hampton Normal and Agricultural Institute
Harlan, Edith
Harlan, Mollie F.
Hartwell, Rosa E.
Hastings, Emily
Hawley, Harriet W.
Hayes, Birchard A.—
  Hayes, Lucy Webb
Hayes, Fanny—
  Hayes, Lucy Webb
Hayes, Lucy Webb—Clippings
Hayes, Lucy Webb—Essays
Hayes, Lucy Webb—Temperance
Hayes, Mary Sherman
Hayes, Rutherford B.—
  Hayes, Lucy Webb
Hayes, Rutherford P.—
  Hayes, Lucy Webb

Hayes, Scott R.—
  Hayes, Lucy Webb
Hayes, Webb C.—
  Hayes, Lucy Webb
Haygood, A. G.
Head, Natt (Mrs.)
Hedges, Henry C. (Mrs.)
Herrick, Kitty M.
Herron, Harriet
Herron, John W.
Herron, Lucy Hayes
Hester, E. Addison (Mrs.)
Hickok, Lillie A.
Hill, Alice
Hiltz, John
Hitt, Mary H. B.
Hoffman, Elizabeth
Holloway, James B.
Holloway, Laura C.
Hopkins, I. A.
Houston, Jane F.
Howells, Elinor M.
Howells, William Dean
Hoyt, F. S. (Mrs.)
Hoyt, John W.
Hudson, B. B. (Mrs.)
Hughes, Kate Duval
Huntington, D.
Hutter, Elizabeth E.

Ide, Harriet E.
Ingham, Mary B.

James, Lucia R.
Jewett, Nelly R.
Jewett, Sam R.
Joel, Louise
Jones, Fannie H.
Jones, Nannie Taylor

Kappa Kappa Gamma
Keeler, Lucy E.
Knapp, W. A.

Laforcade, Amelie
Lamb, Martha J.
Lanahan, John
Laurence, James
Le Duc, William E.
Lewis, Theresa
Lincoln, M. D. (Mrs.)
Little, Caroline M.
Longstreth, Mary Anna
Looker, L. B.
Loring, George B.

Madden, Edward F.
Marcy, E. E. (Mrs.)
Martindale, Emma

Mason, Frances
Mathews, Helen N.
Matthews, Isabella
Matthews, M. A.
Mattock, E. P.
McCabe, H. C.
McCabe, L. D.
McCann, Jennie V.
McCook, Anson G.
McCook, Kate P.
McCready, Sophia
McDowell, Jennie
McDowell, Mary E.
McKell, Jean D.
McKell, Maria
McKell, Phoebe
McLean, Sallie K.
McMeens, Ann C.
Mead, Charles L.
Mellor, Martha
Merrick, Frederick
Meyer, Lucy R.
Miller, E. W.
Mills, Lizzie
Mitchell, Jean
Mitchell, John G.
Mitchell, Laura
Mitchell, Lily
Mohun, Claire Hanson
Monroe, Henrietta L.
Morgan, Kate
Morrill, R. S.
Morse, O. C.
Mosher, Kate E. P.
Moss, Fannie B.
Moss, J. O.
Moss, Mary D.
Myers, Albert J.

Neale, Alice R.
Nicholson, Isabelle E.
Nobel, Lizzie E.
Nordhoff, Lida
Norton, Mary C.

Outrey, Helen Russell

Packard, Anna B.
Parsons, Mary Llewellyn
Pendleton, Alice Kay
Pendleton, Anne I.
Perkins, Sarah M.
Peyton, Jeannie S.
Platt, Susan
Platt, William A.
Pollock, Louise
Pope, Emma
Porter, Martha Day
Potter, Alice K.

Potter, Mary
Ramsey, Anna E.
Rogers, Emma W.
Rollins, E. H. (Mrs.)
Round, William F.
Rowland, Amelia H.
Russell, Caroline
Russell, Fannie E.
Russell, Hattie
Rust, E. L. (Mrs. R. S.)
Schurz Family
Scott, James
Scott, Lizzie W.
Scott, M. Belle
Sharp, Mary A.
Shepard, Joanna M.
Sherman, Cecelia S.
Sherman, Ellen Ewing
Sherman, John
Sherman, Mary S.
Sherman, Rachel
Sherman, William T.
Shoemaker, M. A.
Shoemaker, Samuel M.
Sickels, David
Silver Wedding Anniversary Congratulations
Simpson, Ellen H.
Smith, Edward (Mrs.)
Smith, Emma R.
Smith, Lizzie McK.
Smith, T. C. H.
Snead, Austine
Snead, Fayette C.
Snowden, A. Louden
Sollace, H. L. (Mrs.)
Stevenson, John H.
Stilwell, Kate F.
Strong, R. H.
Swayne Family

Talmage, DeWitt
Taylor, P. W.
Thompson, S. W. (Mrs.)
Thornton, Mary G.
Titcomb, Jennie C.
Toner, J. M.
Tourgee, Emma R.
Tyner, James W. (Mrs.)
Von Koerber, Elise

Waddle, Eleanor
Waite, Alice and Nancy
Waite, Amelia C.
Waite, Mary F.
Ware, I. W.
Ware, Jane G.
Warren, Abby
Watkins, Hepsie
Webb, J. T.

CPSIA information can be obtained
at www.ICGtesting.com
Printed in the USA
BVHW04*1015190918
527934BV00014B/918/P